CHILD OF GOD,

Delight in Him

Art Journaling & Creative Clustering of God's Names

Caranita Wolsieffer

Illustrated by Tony Sobota

WestBow
PRESS®
A DIVISION OF THOMAS NELSON
& ZONDERVAN

All Scripture quotations taken from the Holy Bible, New International Version. Copyright © 1973,1978,1984, International Bible Society. Used by permission of Zondervan Bible Publishers.

WestBow Press books may be ordered through booksellers or by contacting:

WestBow Press
A Division of Thomas Nelson & Zondervan
1663 Liberty Drive
Bloomington, IN 47403
www.westbowpress.com
1 (866) 928-1240

ISBN: 978-1-5127-8587-6 (sc)
ISBN: 978-1-5127-8586-9 (e)

Library of Congress Control Number: 2017907284

Print information available on the last page.

WestBow Press rev. date: 05/17/2017

To my husband, Jim.
Chronic diseases and severe pain have battered you unrelentingly,
but you stand firmly like a lighthouse on the Rock.

When your words came, I ate them; they were my joy and my heart's delight, for I bear your name O Lord God Almighty. I never sat in the company of revelers, never made merry with them; I sat alone because your hand was on me and you had filled me with indignation. Why is my pain unending and my wound grievous and incurable? Will you be to me like a deceptive brook, like a spring that fails?

Jeremiah 15:16-18

Contents

Chapter 5
God's Rest: Priorities

Chapter 6
God's Delight: Hide-and-Seek

Epilogue

Section 4
Seek and Delight in Him

Acknowledgments

In August of 2013, a small group of family and friends committed to pray for a workbook on God's names. The concept of creative clustering came to light almost immediately, and they surrounded this workbook at every stage of its creation. I want to express my heartfelt gratitude to Jim Wolsieffer, Nanette Helm, Tamara Wilhelm, Gianni, Stephany, Anyssa, Raffaele Bruno, John and Marcy Wolsieffer, Becky Wolsieffer Vahle, Lucinda Kesterson, Sandra Sykes, Carol Lawlis, Jeff Hollis, Kevin O'Brien, Kevin Hull, Marsha Ketchen, Jason Casey, Tom and Carmen Mock, Richard and Sandy Lung, Reggie and Carol Hundley, Carolyn Hayes, Jeff Noel, Nancy Breuer, Luca D'Errico, Davide Maglie, and Giuseppe and Paola De Chirico.

This exciting adventure has had some unexpected contributions that have totally transformed the original manuscript of the workbook. My gratitude goes to Eric Schroeder, Senior Publishing Consultant at WestBow Press, for being a part of the initial brainstorming process that turned the workbook into an art journal. Tony Sobota's illustrations will help you praise and pray God's names through the eyes of a child's heart and offer you hours of coloring enjoyment. To our daughter, Stephany, thank you for your "Graceful Lament" and your vitality. Your well of love and hope never runs dry. To Janice R. S. Looper, thank you for being you in "That Way."

My deepest gratitude goes to Ed Roark, deceased April 2016 after a four-year battle with a brain tumor. Ed was more than a brother to us. His daughter, Heather Roark Van Gorp, donated a tithe from the Roark Trust Fund without knowing about this workbook project. We received the funds the day after we signed the contract with WestBow. Thank you, Ed, for reaching out in love across death's temporary barrier. Thank you, Heather, for following your dad's example of caring for others while facing so much personal loss in such a short time.

I couldn't have started this journey without the understanding hearts and commitment of Mark and Lisa Pruden. Thank you for walking by my side through the dark times and showing me the delightful path of living grace. And last of all, thanks to my "sis", Charlene Slayton, for your faithful friendship and sense of humor. Joy's treasures for you are like pearls, symbolic of precious healing from life's wounds.

May the only true God be glorified from the first to the last page of *Child of God, Delight in Him!* He will do immeasurably more than all we ask or imagine.

Introduction

Coloring Maps to My Father's Heart

As a missionary's wife, church leader, and Christian counselor in the public arena, where could I find shelter to work through my own complicated trauma and mourn significant losses? My childlike faith had shattered, and a dark, endless hole threatened to engulf me. From the bottom of the pit, I could still see a tiny ray of light. Would help arrive in time? But what I feared most came true. Job's three friends appeared and rolled large stones of unrealistic expectations precariously close to the small opening. They sat down on those stones, and their words drifted down to me.

"Christians must always rejoice in suffering!"

"Just sing and pray harder! Crying only makes it worse!"

"Surely you did something to deserve this—repent!"

"Christian leaders must not give in to self-pity. Since you are depressed, maybe you aren't a Christian."

Their words mingled with my tears, and I slipped deeper in the sinking sand. David's psalm of distress (Psalm 69) became my personal reality.

Added to the suffering was my intense longing to find my way home to my Father's heart. Armed with a light blue colored pencil and a small notebook, I started searching for God's names in the Bible. Two years later I had colored a path from Genesis to Revelation, one name and one page at a time. During that time God also sent a small "Elihu group" (Job 32–37) that climbed down into the pit of distress to listen and cry with me, to love and challenge me, to help me through the suffering instead of letting me deny or avoid it.

During these twenty-five years, my search for God's names has expanded into a treasure hunt through ten Bibles in English and Italian. Each Bible has been personalized and given to our children, grandchildren, and a few friends. I am presently working on the next Bible for our fourth grandchild. My small notebook of an alphabetical list of God's names transformed itself into an accordion-like experience.[1] Filled with living breath, it expanded into five hundred pages of computer-generated charts accompanied by questions. Overwhelmed by a study that wasn't exhaustive but was exhausting, I attempted to compress the accordion inward for a women's Bible study. For two years we studied His attributes, prayed His names, and memorized Scripture.[2] Blessings and Christlike transformation became obvious to our friends and families.

---

[1] God's names/names of God are concise expressions that are inclusive of the names, attributes, descriptions, images, metaphors, and prototypes of the theophany of the Trinity.

[2] After twenty-five years of searching, coloring, and mapping God's names, I am compelled to capitalize the pronouns (He, His, Him, Theirs, Me, My, etc.) of the Trinity. As a child, I remember the sense of awe instilled in

Passionately motivated by the success of the women's Bible study, I pulled out the bellows of the accordion once again and started a chronological list of His names. I felt convinced that if I could go through the Bible, page by page, and not miss even one name and its context, the study would grow in significance. New elements such as *who, when,* and *where* proved fascinating. But I raised a white flag of surrender at Isaiah 33:21 and sat down in awe before His name as *Mighty One, Majestic One* (NASB). The mind of a child can dream an impossible dream but not understand how to make it come true. I set all the study material aside to collect dust on a shelf.

More personal losses, a major move, and my husband's long-standing battles with physical disabilities, diseases, and chronic pain (a C4–C5 cervical fracture, four chronically debilitating diseases, a spinal cord stimulator implant, multiple traumatic surgeries for a urostomy, and battles with continuous infections) reawakened the struggle between my problem-solving mind and my broken heart. With Jacob-like force, I wrestled with God and with men.[3] What obstacles keep us from "rejoicing with those who rejoice and weeping with those who weep"?[4] Is it more difficult for the rejoicing to weep with those who weep or for the mourners to rejoice with those who rejoice? How do we unite the two opposite worlds of suffering and delight? How do we get them into the same room for an open dialogue? What would they say to each other? How do we harmonize what we know about God in our heads with how we experience Him in our hearts? How do we connect that inner channel so that the God of all grace, who saves us by grace, can also sanctify us by grace? How do God's names fit into all this? Better yet, how do I get God's names to fit in anywhere?

At dawn on May 25, 2013, my invisible tension became palpable in a prayer room at the European Leadership Conference (ELF) in Wisla, Poland, an unfamiliar land where I knew absolutely no one. Tears flowed as I wrote an anonymous prayer card. "Please pray for me as I walk through personal grief. As I struggle with acceptance, please pray that I will find comfort like Mary Magdalene before an empty tomb. Pray that my personal relationship with my precious *Rabboni* deepens. Pray that I will give His message to broken hearts. Thank you." Within hours the God of all comfort led me to the women's Bible study, where I met two teachers (sisters) and a room monitor, all three from my childhood home of Indianapolis, Indiana. He whispered my name, and I cried out, *"Rabboni!"* He delighted me on my birthday.

The following evening, I had supper with the mentor whom I had chosen months prior to ELF. Surrounded by all the noise and confusion of over seven hundred participants, I sat face-to-face with Nanette Helm, one of the sisters from Indianapolis. God arranged even this serendipitous meeting to condense years of searching into one hour of heart-to-heart sharing. My journal entry briefly records Nanette's godly advice as we talked about my passion for God's names.

---

me when I saw His pronouns capitalized. Even in the face of a logical and linguistic explanation for lowercase, I choose to honor the infinite depths of God's names as my creative responses to Him in this workbook.

[3] Genesis 32:24–32.

[4] Romans 12:15.

- Prayer: Form a prayer team in America. The closer you get to completing the project, the less you will be able to bear the growing resistance.
- Perspective: You aren't doing this for yourself but for the younger generation that needs to know God in His essence of *I AM*.
- Make it colorfully condensed: Your perfectionism and headwork expanded a compilation of God's names out of control, so now listen to His heart and yours.

Her last and most important advice surprised both of us: select a core Scripture to guide you. As I shared my meditation on John 20 and Mary Magdalene at the tomb, her eyes widened with recognition. "The anonymous prayer card about grief and Mary Magdalene is yours, isn't it? A small group of us have been praying intensely over your request since you left it in the prayer room. It deeply touched all of us." It became obvious to both of us that, while the Christian Counseling Network motivated my presence at the ELF conference, God used it to arrange unexpected encounters to call me back to His names!

A few days after my return from Poland, I had the following dream, which revealed a significant trust issue still blocking my heart.

> My husband, a counseling client, and I are in a classroom taking notes from a counseling supervisor. The supervisor and client joke and laugh together until the client's laughter erupts into uncontrollable crying. Unable to talk because of her emotional pain, she writes the name *Raffaele* (Raphael—"healing God") on her notebook. The supervisor gently asks, "Are you suffering so intensely that you can't even say my name?" Her cry deepens into sobs, and she starts rocking back and forth. The supervisor wraps his arms around her and tells her to reach out her hand and touch the wall in front of her each time she rocks forward. The wall has two opposing forces: one is wavy with bright, living colors; the other is rough, with very sharp-pointed tacks. Raphael (healing God) lovingly confronts her by saying, "This is reality."

I abruptly reawakened to my own reality to ponder the timing and meaning of such emotional images. It proved to be a prelude to the next stage of deterioration of my husband's health and major changes in his care. Could I trust God to heal my inner pain when He had chosen not to heal any of my husband's physical disabilities? Did I want constant contact with a wall that invited me with beautiful colors and then punctured me? To my gratitude, a psychologist friend who had been helping me cope with my stress from caregiving began to explore my resistance to writing. He pestered me with questions like, "What are the obstacles that keep you from pulling your book toward you? How much energy do you lose by pushing it away? What are your fears? What keeps your head and heart divided? What would your head and heart say to each other if they could sit down together in the same room?"

While waiting for answers, I pulled out my colored pencils to color butterflies. My soul quieted itself in God's presence as I contemplated one of His delicate symbols of profound transformation. "Be still, and know that I am God."[5] In this silence the eyes of my heart glimpsed a deeper meaning that unites joy and suffering in the Lord's Supper. The pleasant aromas of fresh bread and sweet wine call me joyfully into His presence at the same time my heart is pierced with the images of Christ's atrocious suffering on a rugged cross. Joy and suffering do talk to each other in the same room, around a table. "Let us fix our eyes on Jesus, the author and perfecter of our faith, who for the joy set before him endured the cross, scorning its shame … Consider him …"[6] How would Jesus describe His joy intertwined with suffering? How did He keep joy set before Him while on the cross? What helps me consider Him despite personal suffering?

Consider comes from Latin, and its synonyms include *contemplate, examine, scrutinize, study, meditate, reason, reflect, chew over, think deliberately, turn over in one's mind.* The Latin stem *sidus, sidereral* turns our eyes heavenward to contemplate stars and sky. Consider Him, the Creator of all, coming down to touch our wall of reality, despising and pushing back against the shame of sin and the worse torture imaginable, yet rejoicing to restore the Godhead's relationship with us. *Considering* Him balances mind with heart, thoughts with emotions, knowledge with delight. He invites us to look in, look around, look up, and look beyond.

Will I accept His invitation to bring my whole self to His banquet of names? I have known (head) Him better through His names, but am I delighting (heart) in each one of them? Do I have joy in His presence as I go through pain in the present? On August 1, 2013, Nanette Helm surprised me with an email: "I have been praying for the work to flow through his presence and power. I hope you are delighting in him through each name. Praying also for you and your husband to see the fruit of your labor—his help in life's struggles." We had not had any contact since the ELF Conference in Poland, so what a surprise to see that she underlined the core reason for the search, "delighting in him through each name." Only the Holy Spirit knew that my long-term inability to *delight in Him* lay in a massive rubble of shattered childhood trust. How did Nanette know that God had just asked me, a few days prior to her message, "For years you searched to know Me through My names, but will you now continue the search to delight in Me?" My curiosity scampered to my dictionary of synonyms. "Delight" combines the two emotions of joy and surprise. "Then will I go to the altar of God, to God, my joy and my delight."[7] Once again there are two opposing forces: a symbol of sacrifice (altar) and an emotion of joyful delight. Did I trust Him enough to keep putting myself on His altar? As I pulled the study of His names off the shelf and blew away the dust, I begged my healing God to delight me.

A small group of Christian family members and friends circled around the project to energize and protect it. At that point my heart perceived a theme of light and darkness as I

---

5 Psalm 46:10.
6 Hebrews 12:2–3.
7 Psalm 43:4.

read how Mary Magdalene sobbed before a black, empty tomb. Curiosity grabbed me again. How many of God's names focus on light? To whom did God reveal Himself with this group of names? I scanned my compiled list of God's names, and an *aha* moment flashed before me. Like a child, I squealed with delight at the connection. A providential Internet search for synonyms then transported me to a colorful, concise structure that I had seen several years before in a seminar led by Jeff Noel. Further connections occurred. What would happen if I were to combine that kind of structure with God's names of light? Time stood still. I could hardly breathe as I mind mapped God's names of light.

Before my eyes appeared a flexible, colorful structure that compressed, yet expanded; contained, yet perpetuated, simplified, yet mystified. During the next thirteen months, thirty-two clusters expanded to include over eight hundred names of God, seeds to plant, Bible verses for practical application, push-back points, invisible tension areas, enemy territory, and antonyms. Each cluster developed gradually after multiple prayerful revisions. An underlying musical rhythm and unending shades of colors accompanied me. The awe of His majesty burst into kaleidoscopes and fireworks, delighting my childlike curiosity as I mixed and matched His names. Pure delight dawned every morning as He walked by my side to explore maps and to dream impossible dreams. He gently restored my childhood trust, piece by piece.

One desire intensified during this time—if I could only set to music the delight I heard in my heart while creatively clustering God's names. When I expressed this desire to my husband, he took me into his arms and said, "Sweetheart, God has a special instrument waiting for you in heaven. It is a large, semicircular organ with layered keyboards. Each key has one of His names on it. He will ask you to compose never-ending songs for choirs of angels and saints. You will be able to select different combinations of key names to bring us into the presence of His majesty. The Lion and the Lamb will reveal unknown names and unending colors that will delight us for all eternity!" Tears flowed down my face as I embraced his pain-racked body and rejoiced that we can serve our healing God in the light of the reality of suffering.

Section 1

Unpacking the Maps

Hear, O Israel: The Lord our God, the Lord is one. Love the Lord your God with all your heart and with all your soul and with all your strength. These commandments that I give you today are to be upon your hearts. Impress them on your children. Talk about them when you sit at home and when you walk along the road, when you lie down and when you get up.

Deuteronomy 6:4-7
Matthew 22:37-40

Connections: Names, Maps, Colors, Images

You just won tickets for your dream trip on one condition: you can travel toward but not reach your destination. Excited? Disappointed? Would you still pack your suitcase and leave, or would you stay home? Would you start out but then eventually turn back? Exploring God's names is like winning an awesome trip and knowing that the destination is beyond reach. No pilgrim has ever hoisted a flag on the summit of God's being and His names, for the world itself can't contain all the books about Him. He is life and the giver of life. How could we ever bind into a book or enclose into a building the very one who declared, "As the heavens are higher than the earth, so are my ways higher than yours and my thoughts than your thoughts"?[8] Dr. Herbert Lockyer emphasizes that the infinite astounds our finite minds.[9] So what compels us to inch upwards to unreachable heights, and how could this workbook accompany you?

Child of God, Delight in Him doesn't offer in-depth, theological studies of God's names and attributes. There is no attempt to separate the names of the Old and New Testaments or to group the names under God, Son, and Holy Spirit. Many authors have already explored the depths and symbolism of His names in Hebrew, Greek, and Aramaic. British scholar and preacher James Large wrote his classic *Titles and Symbols of Christ* in 1880 for the poor and for families with young children. His searching meditations have been revised and reprinted several times. More recent authors like Hebert Lockyer, Elmer Town, and Ann Spangler integrate ancient biblical customs, language, and meanings with practical applications for the challenges of modern cultures. Systematic theology authors like Millard J. Erickson, Wayne Grudem, and Robert D. Bell have been my constant companions through all these years.

Child of God, Delight in Him does open new pathways by offering

1. a dynamic process of associative clustering and color coding to explore the Bible for God's names;
2. creative connections of God's names, attributes, descriptions, images, metaphors, prototypes, and anthropomorphisms;
3. practical applications of God's names for personal growth in prayer, meditation, memorization, Bible study, and worship;
4. integration between knowledge and personal relationships (head and heart);
5. encouragement to trust God when He seems distant and silent;
6. mental stability in the face of suffering or emotional distress;
7. personal incentive to create more maps, write meditations/prayers, and renew meaningful worship.

---

[8] Isaiah 55:8–9.

[9] Herbert Lockyer, *All the Divine Names and Titles in the Bible* (Grand Rapids: Zondervan, 1975), 90.

Provisions for the Journey

Metaphorically speaking, you will find the following provisions for the trip: walking stick (stability); trekking shoes (life application); compass (reference points); seeds (progress); backpack (tools); traveler's journal (connection); and serendipities (delights).

Walking Stick (Stability)

The walking stick is an alphabetical list of creative clusters that includes common denominators. Think of a specific need or concern in this moment of your life and then select a title or a common denominator of names that seems to resonate. Take the time to become familiar with your chosen map and decide if those names and seeds can help you grow in your relationships with God and others. If not, return to the alphabetical list and choose a different map. You will soon discover that the titles of the maps and their common denominators are subjective. You could eventually give your own titles that reflect your spiritual experience. As you pray and meditate on God's names in respect to your needs and concerns, you will regain stability in your daily walk. You can return to the alphabetical list after you finish a map or whenever you want to explore new territory.

Trekking Shoes (Life Application)

So how do you get God's names to flow from mind to heart and into daily living? One way is to put on sturdy trekking shoes and walk persistently over the rough terrain of doubts and questions. John Piper emphasizes that it takes profound questions and ceaseless searching for the answers to find the true God and understand His truth.[10] Trekking shoes must be worn with the same respectful and submissive attitude as that found in the Book of Job and in the Psalms. The search for hidden treasure along the way leads to the fear (awe, worship) of the Lord.[11]

Compass (Reference Points)

Scripture is the only compass to keep us traveling in the right direction.

➢ "Describe His Names" and "Love and Live His Names" are two Scripture indexes that clarify the underlying scriptural motivation for knowing and delighting in God's names.

➢ "Seek and Delight in Him" offers a concise Scripture index with over eight hundred of God's names, attributes, descriptions, images, and prototypes.

---

[10] John Piper, *Think: The Life of the Mind and the Love of God* (Wheaton: Crossway, 2010).
[11] Proverbs 2:1–8.

> Your own personal Bible is the most essential reference point. If you can develop the habit of consulting several translations of the Bible for God's names, your search will be enriched.

Seeds (Progress)

You might decide to start your journey by consulting the "Alphabetical List of Seeds to Plant." The seeds help identify the values that are important to you. Values are principles (ethics, morals) that a person cherishes immeasurably and then publically commits himself to believe, think, feel, and act consistently. Values give a purpose to live and a reason to die, if necessary. To grow from seed, to plant, and to mature into fruit takes time and God's loving care. Those around you should see your progress, not your perfection.[12]

Backpack (Tools)

Drs. Tom and Beverly Rodgers teach the following concept: "Research shows that repeatedly thinking of God as a positive, loving figure can change the brain's functioning. The limbic system is healed by repetition and experience. Helping people replace negative thoughts with positive ones can create the flow of beneficial brain chemicals, while experiencing healing conversations and interactions in their relationships can restore the wounded brain."[13] If you have experienced deep hurts and/or trauma, praying and meditating on God's names with a variety of tools can restore wholeness.

> The principal tool used in this workbook is mind mapping. I prefer to call it *creative clustering*. If you are seeing it for the first time, you may feel a little intimidated by all the lines and disconnected boxes. But once you grasp the concept, you will be able to interrelate God's names in ways that open new channels for prayer and worship. You will also increase your recall of His names since creative clustering processes information by connecting words, images, logic, and color. You can select your own colors, interact with the clusters, and personalize them. (An e-book version of *Child of God, Delight in Him* can be downloaded as a guide.)

> The "Overview of a Creative Cluster" and its accompanying "Model of a Creative Cluster" briefly explain how to unpack the clusters. No two clusters are alike, but they do share a basic structure. If you need more information on mind mapping in general, you will find an Internet resource in the bibliography.

---

[12] 1 Timothy 4:15.

[13] Beverly Rodgers and Tom Rodgers, "Neurological insights into emotional reactivity and relational conflict," *Christian Counseling Connection*, Vol.19, Issue 4, December 2013.

➢ The use of concordances, dictionaries, and a thesaurus explores never-ending connections of meanings and a greater depth of symbolism.

➢ If you transfer the names and Bible references from the maps onto white and/or colored index cards with colored pencils or pens, it will increase your comprehension of how they all interrelate, thereby increasing memorization.

Traveler's Journal (Connection)

What makes people turn their heads for a second look and exclaim, "Wow, unreal?" Going viral seems to tap into the desire to post the most unusual, hilarious, or breathtaking idea to capture the attention of complete strangers. God went viral long before the Internet: the first rainbow after a flood; an unconsumed burning bush; a dry path through a major river bed; a talking donkey who saw an angel; a proud king transformed into a cow; a humble King asleep in a manger; angels shutting lions' mouths; tied-up men relaxing in a fiery furnace; the superhero dead on a cross; a supposed ghost eating fish; an elevator ride on a cloud. The Bible has its own Internet of head-turning events. Do we still know how to connect to them?

On the opposite page of each map, you will find your own traveler's journal so you can talk with God about His names. "Creative Responses to God, Jesus, and the Holy Spirit" encourages you to color, design, glue images/pictures, journal, write songs or poems, and ask questions. Journaling has also proven beneficial for emotional healing.[14] If possible, create a small group to share the highlights of one another's journeys. The experience of connecting to others will transform His names into perpetual, three-dimensional kaleidoscopes.

Serendipities (Delights)

It is said that a tourist can visit Rome in three days, buy a T-shirt, and hurry on to the next city on his itinerary. A pilgrim can visit Rome every day for five years and still not learn about all its monuments and history. Eugene Peterson reminds us that a tourist-like attitude, with its fast pace, has permeated even our churches. That kind of attitude won't produce mature disciples.[15] It takes the commitment of a pilgrim to unpack the maps. Those who persevere will be blessed with serendipities during the routine tasks of each day.

Symbolic meanings are tucked into the seven illustrations of "Carrie's Joy." Her feelings of awe, hurt, gratitude, impatience, perseverance, love, trust, and delight could be anyone's life story. Bringing them alive in your own colors could unlock both pleasant and painful

---

[14] James W. Pennebaker, *Writing to Heal: A Guided Journal for Recovering from Trauma and Emotional Upheaval* (Oakland: New Harbinger, 2004).

[15] Eugene Peterson, *A Long Obedience in the Same Direction: Discipleship in an Instant Society* (Downers Grove: InterVarsity Press, 2000).

memories. I hope that you will connect God's names to those areas of your life that need His tender touch while you reflect and color. He will delight you as you go through the suffering.

God will also delight you in ways that you can't even imagine if you venture out to create your own maps. You will discover "the treasures of darkness, riches stored in secret places."[16] Here are just a few tips to get started making maps.

> Select about twenty-five of your favorite names of God, divide them into a core and four wings, and color the basic structure.

> Identify a specific need in your life, a relative's life, or a friend's life. Then select the names of God that seem to answer that need.

> Find the names that you think have a common theme or relationship.

> Select a biblical character and search for the names that God used to reveal Himself to that person.

> Select a psalm (or your favorite chapter of the Bible) and explore the names that the Holy Spirit chose to reveal in that passage.

> Select an entire book of the Bible to explore to whom, when, and how God revealed Himself to the people in that book.

> Choose a theme that is relevant to your daily walk with God (dignity, perseverance, obedience, trust, etc.) and then select the names of God that harmonize with your theme.

By creating and unpacking clusters, you will discover a dynamic, inductive Bible study with infinite possibilities. Combine a child's delight in surprises with an adult's hunger for significance while remembering that God's names can't be confined to anyone's book. May this exciting journey influence your relationships with God, others, and yourself. The path that leads home to your Father's heart will radiate colors and emotions that you've never imagined. What more could you want or need?

Invisible Tension (IT) and Push Back

These two areas of the creative clusters require an in-depth explanation that follows in "Transformation."

---

[16] Isaiah 45:3.

Alphabetical List of Creative Clusters

Title	Common Denominators
Ageless Splendor	(eternity/immortality)
Altar of Forgiveness	(forgiveness/Priest/offerings)
Anchored in Hope	(hope/guide/way)
Be Still and Know	(Deity/mightiness/transcendent)
Became Like Us	(Son/Man/incarnation)
Called to Be	(Servant/roles)
Child's Prayer	(variety of names)
Christlikeness	(person of Holy Spirit)
Effective Ministry	(gifts and fruit of Holy Spirit)
Father's Footsteps	(God as Father)
Face-to-Face	(refuge/shelter/temple)
Fragrance of Life	(quintessence of God)
Garden of Discipleship	(seed/root/vine)
Gracious Promise	(grace/mercy/compassion)
Hidden Treasure	(gift/riches/mystery)
In the Beginning	(light/fire/glory)
Marvelous in Our Eyes	(redemption/reconciliation/salvation)
Model of Suffering	(rejection/humiliation/crucifixion)
Pathfinder	(variety of names)
Peacemaker	(Shepherd/peace/rest)
Rock-solid Faith	(faith/foundation/rock)
Rooted in Love	(covenant/unfailing love)
Run with Perseverance	(variety of names)
Secret of Being Content	(banquet/bread/water)
Servant's Heart	(Servant/kingdom/throne)
Set Apart by Design	(holiness/righteousness/anointed)
Spiritual Warfare	(leader/head/armor)
Surprised by Joy	(joy/delight/inheritance)
The Way of Truth	(Prophet/truth/judge/justice)
Umbrella of Fellowship	(dwell/God of/immanent)
Valley of Decision	(cross/Lamb/witness/overcome)
Your Will Be Done	(King/Lord/Prince)

Life Application Questions

The following questions serve only as catalysts to encourage you to put on your trekking shoes. You might want to use the extra space that follows to write your own questions as you listen to your thoughts and feelings.

How can I breathe, talk, and walk each name so that others will know and delight in Him?

How does knowing/delighting in God's names change me?

How does knowing/delighting in God's names make me more Christlike?

How does knowing/delighting in God's names change my relationship with my family? With the church family? With friends? With coworkers?

How does knowing/delighting in God's names change how I reconcile the reality of pain and suffering with my desire for peace and joy?

Who or what am I pushing back against in my own human nature or in this fallen world? How does God help me push back with the power in His names?

Have I ever considered to whom and when God revealed each of His names?

How would my approach to others change if I would truly listen to their struggles and then ask myself which of His names might be an entry point into their personal lives?

Which ten names for God are special to me, and how do they speak to my heart?

If I could dance to God's names, which ten would I pick, and how would my nonverbal expressions help me worship God with all my heart, soul, mind, and strength?

If I could compose music, which ten names of God would I choose, and what melodies do I hear with those names?

If I could pick gifts to give to myself/family/friends that somehow symbolize God's names, how would I go about picking God's names and/or the gifts for myself/each person?

How would praying God's names help me relate simultaneously to a rejoicing person and a grieving person, each at his/her own level?

When someone who is struggling falls into a faith crisis, what do I do or say? How would knowing God's names change my approach?

When someone admits that they don't/can't believe in a God who allows suffering, how would my answers change if I were to choose a few of His names to pray silently and then possibly share with this seeker?

How much do I truly allow myself and others to lament when brokenhearted? Which of God's names would help me open this vital channel of communication?

How much do I truly allow myself and others to delight in God's presence? Which of God's names would help me open this vital channel of communication?

How much of my day is packed with work, activities, and social media? How much silence do I incorporate into my meditations and worship? Which names of God would help me quiet my soul?

What do I think, feel, and do when I hear coworkers/friends/family use God's name in vain? How would increasing reverence/awe/fear of God's names change my attitude and any passivity?

Two biblical characters (Jacob and Manoah) wanted to know the name of the angel of the Lord. The angel answered them, "Why do you ask my name?" Manoah was told that the name was beyond understanding. Why do you want to know God's names, and what will you do with them?

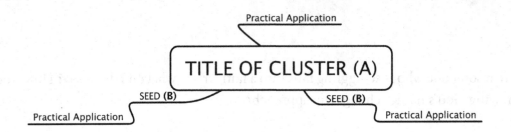

Practical Application

TITLE OF CLUSTER (A)

SEED **(B)**

SEED **(B)**

Practical Application

Practical Application

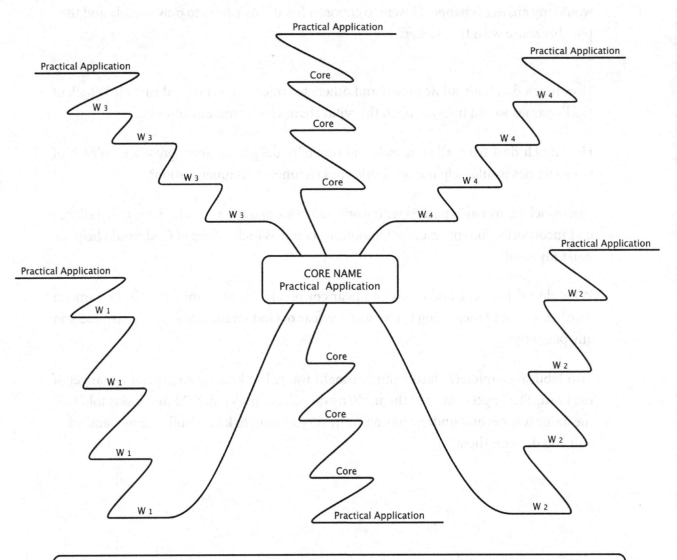

Practical Application

Core

Practical Application

Practical Application

W 3

Core

W 4

W 3

Core

W 4

W 3

W 4

W 3

W 4

Practical Application

Practical Application

W 1

CORE NAME
Practical Application

W 2

W 1

Core

W 2

W 1

Core

W 2

W 1

Core

W 2

Practical Application

INVISIBLE TENSION **(I.T.)** **(D)**
(essential area for understanding clusters and represented symbolically by space)

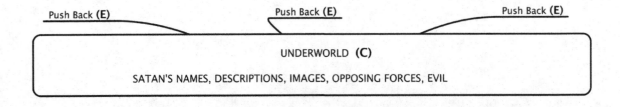

Push Back **(E)**

Push Back **(E)**

Push Back **(E)**

UNDERWORLD **(C)**

SATAN'S NAMES, DESCRIPTIONS, IMAGES, OPPOSING FORCES, EVIL

ANTONYMS OF SEEDS

Overview of a Creative Cluster

Title (A) (future: who we strive to be)
Each title has a symbolic meaning relative to its cluster.

Seeds (B) (future: who we strive to be)
Seeds are biblical principles, values, and ethics rooted in biblical truth. Buried out of sight, spiritual seeds require a slow process of transformation (sanctification). Seeds come with a warning: We will reap destruction if we sow to please the sinful nature. We are to sow to please the Spirit and not grow weary with this God-given task.

Identify the enemy (C) (past: who we were)
Ephesians 6:10–20 underlines the necessity to identify the enemy first. Each of the thirty-two creative clusters introduces an associated antithesis of Satan. Satan's names have limited acclaim compared to God's breathtaking revelation of His names. The antonyms represent the enemy's weapons and tactics to crush God's seeds.

Invisible Tension (IT) (D) (present: who we are)
(essential for understanding the clusters and represented symbolically by space)
An invisible tension point resides in all of us, creating an inner struggle. The good often eludes us while the wrong invades us. We groan in our weaknesses for the Spirit's help. God's names provide divine strength for us to put off the old man and put on the new one constantly. We are to stand firm and persevere, no matter what.

Push back (E) (present: who we are)
Each cluster proposes three foundation verses to push back against Satan's intent to capture us as prisoners of war. Matthew 4:1–11 teaches us that Christ didn't argue, discuss, or debate with the enemy. God's Word is living, active, and sharper than any double-edged sword. There are certain times and circumstances in which praying Scripture is much more effective than our own words.

Core names
Most of the clusters have one designated core name in large print at the center of the page. Additional core names have been arranged subjectively, from bottom to top, to facilitate flowing conversational prayer from one name to the next. Consulting respective Scriptures for each name deepens our prayer life and relationship with the only true God.

Wings (W$_1$, W$_2$, W$_3$, W$_4$, etc.)

The wings graphically connect to the core names or remain in flight. These additional names of God have been arranged to flow from lower left to lower right, then upper left to upper right. The flexibility of mind mapping permits shifting wings to accommodate individual preferences for mental associations and memorization. These names are also located in the alphabetical list.

Practical application Bible verses

Practical application Bible verses have been associated with the titles (A), the seeds (B), the core names, and with each wing. They answer the question, "How do His names change me?"

Alphabetical List of Seeds to Plant

(values/priorities)

acceptance (Peacemaker)

altruism (Secret of Being Content)

authenticity (Set Apart by Design)

being (Fragrance of Life)

be strong (Spiritual Warfare)

charitable love (Servant's Heart)

clarity (Called to Be)

choices (Pathfinder)

commitment (Rooted in Love)

compassion (Became Like Us)

competency (Called to Be)

confession (Altar of Forgiveness)

confidence (Rock-solid Faith)

connection (Fragrance of Life)

consequences (Pathfinder)

courage (Anchored in Hope)

delightful devotion(s) (The Way of Truth)

differentiation (Be Still and Know)

dialogue (Umbrella of Fellowship)

dignity (Umbrella of Fellowship)

discernment (Pathfinder)

empathy (Became Like Us)

encouragement (Anchored in Hope)

endurance (Valley of Decision)

ethics (Hidden Treasure)

expectations (Ageless Splendor)

fruit of the Spirit (Effective Ministry)

gifts of the Spirit (Effective Ministry)

giving heart (Garden of Discipleship)

godliness (Set Apart by Design)

godly fear (Be Still and Know)

goodness (Secret of Being Content)

humility (Servant's Heart)

incredible identity (The Way of Truth)

integrity (Father's Footsteps)

joy (Model of Suffering)

knowledge (In the Beginning)

love of Christ (Christlikeness)

maturity (Run with Perseverance)

meditation (Model of Suffering)

mind of Christ (Christlikeness)

noble character (Gracious Promise)

oneness of Christ (Christlikeness)

obedience (Rooted in Love)

patience (Servant's Heart)

priorities (Hidden Treasure)

promises (Ageless Splendor)

quietness (Run with Perseverance)

reality (Be Still and Know)

receiving heart (Garden of Discipleship)

reconciliation (Marvelous in Our Eyes)

rejoice (Surprised by Joy)

reliance (Rock-solid Faith)

renewal (Face to Face)

repentance (Altar of Forgiveness)

requests (Your Will be Done)

resolution (Father's Footsteps)

respect (Your Will Be Done)

rest (Face to Face)

restoration (Marvelous in Our Eyes)

run towards (Spiritual Warfare)

security (Father's Footsteps)

self-denial (Rooted in Love)

share (Surprised by Joy)

simplicity (Child's Prayer)

sing (Surprised by Joy)

significance (Model of Suffering)

stability (Rock-solid Faith)

stand firm (Spiritual Warfare)

submission (Your Will Be Done)

tears (Valley of Decision)
tenderness (Gracious Promise)
thanksgiving (Secret of Being Content)
time (Fragrance of Life)
trust (Face to Face)
understanding (In the Beginning)
unity (Peacemaker)
values (Hidden Treasure)

vision (Called to Be)
waiting (Run with Perseverance)
wisdom (In the Beginning)
witness (Valley of Decision)
wonderment (Child's Prayer)
worship (Surprised by Joy)
yielding (Peacemaker)

Transformation

We read C. S. Lewis's books about Narnia to our children and watched the movies with our grandchildren countless times. The toy chest had a special corner for Narnia's action figures, costumes, pop-up books, and soundtracks. With plastic swords held high, we courageously ran down the hallway into battle, screaming, "For Narnia and for Aslan!" One of our grandsons included Aslan in his prayers, right after the Father, the Son, and the Holy Spirit. If you have journeyed into Narnia, you can probably share similar experiences and favorite scenes. One scene, however, was missed by some people. Did you see it?

Four siblings tumble out of an old wardrobe and fall on the floor. The land of Narnia lies behind them, and the professor stands over them. He urges them to share their story and throws a baseball to Peter. The film credits scroll on the screen, the music intensifies, and people put on their coats to leave. Left all alone, only my daughter and I saw the epilogue to *The Lion, the Witch, and the Wardrobe*. Little Lucy tiptoes toward the wardrobe with expectation on her face. As she reaches for the handle, the professor startles her from his vantage point on the windowsill. He gives her the bad news that she can't return by the same way. He has already tried. Walking hand in hand out of the room, he urges Lucy to keep her eyes open. The wardrobe door swings open a few inches. The resurrected Aslan roars. Now it is finished.

Just like the *Narnia* film, the Gospel of John adds an epilogue that could be missed. The film credits roll, the music swells, and John concludes, "These (miracles) are written that you may believe that Jesus is the Christ, the Son of God, and that by believing you may have life in his name." People could put on their coats and hurry to their next appointment. But some fishermen stumble onto a beach with one more miraculous load of fish. The risen Lion of Judah metaphorically tosses a ball to Peter: "Do you love me?" Christ intentionally created an invisible tension point by asking the same question and giving the same command three times. John tells us that it hurt Peter.

That same question and hurt erupted into my life during a two-year spiritual crisis. As if my personal struggles with childhood trauma weren't enough, our advisory board resigned, and a church wanted to terminate their support. My husband decided to return to the States for furlough, leaving me the responsibility of managing a crisis telephone ministry and helping our daughter finish her last year of high school. Four months into my husband's absence, solitude and sadness surrounded me one night, and I begged God for help. I had slipped into a restless sleep until about 1:30 a.m., when a voice awakened me with, "Do you love Me more than these? Feed My sheep." A deep sense of awe accompanied me as I grabbed my Bible and repeatedly read John 21. But then, like gnawing termites, questions ate away at my peace.

"How can my husband feed the sheep if we don't have financial support from the churches?"

"Who am I to feed the sheep since my faith has shattered?"

"Will my husband think that I had a nervous breakdown when I tell him about the voice in the night?"

Within hours of the experience, my husband called me for our weekly appointment. After addressing the usual needs and concerns, I took a deep breath and said, "I have something to tell you." He started crying before I could finish. After a long silence, he shared what happened to him at the same time I had heard the voice. The very church that was going to terminate our support invited him to a weekly Bible study. The preacher asked everyone to open their Bibles to John 21, and a lively discussion followed about why and how to feed God's sheep.

After listening to differing opinions, my husband finally spoke up: "I was called to feed the sheep in Italy twenty-five years ago. A shepherd never abandons his sheep, not even one, and no matter the personal cost. Feeding sheep in a foreign culture makes a shepherd even more vulnerable to unexpected attacks. I renew our commitment to remain in Italy as long as God calls us. He has made a way so far, and I trust Him to continue." We both fell silent as we pondered the extraordinary timing of events. The voice experience of John 21 was like watching a locked door swing open.

Invisible Tension (IT)

After such a powerful testimony, this next paragraph should have been full of wonderful accomplishments. But for weeks, everything that I wrote seemed superficial and clumsy. What would it take to move beyond my writer's block? More reflection? More prayers? More dark chocolate and espresso coffee? A longer walk? I chose this last option since it usually helps to walk and talk with the Someone who asks me, "What things?"[17] Just like the two sad disciples on the way to Emmaus, I had missed some things.

The things in my case were more gnawing termites: "How can we feed God's sheep if Jim has a debilitating disability? How can I tell others how to unpack the IT area on the maps if I am, once again, avoiding my own pain? Why are others healed, but not Jim? Why does their rejoicing often feel like coarse sandpaper grating on my emotional wounds? Since God called us to feed His sheep, couldn't He have equipped us with good health to do it? "How long, o Lord, how long?" There are no answers, but my vulnerability escorts me into IT terrain that I would much rather avoid.

For that matter, everyone tries to avoid the black holes of suffering and loss. No one likes being disappointed, hurt, and abandoned. Sadly, the Holocaust, wars, natural disasters, accidents, cancer, birth defects, sexual abuse, and terrorist attacks like September 11 are parts of the brutal reality of life, not exceptions to it. In her presentation, "Fellowship of His Suffering: Ground Zero" (2010), Dr. Diane Langberg proposes that redemption becomes powerless if Christians try to cover the indescribable suffering of atrocities and trauma. She underlines two essential priorities for healing: 1) Worship the resurrected Lamb on His throne,

---

[17] Luke 24:19.

which brings humility and repentance; 2) Apply God's truth to everyday living, no matter what happens. Dr. Langberg's invitation creates the same tension that Jesus created in Peter and that Paul creates in us. Do we know and love the resurrected Christ so much that everything else becomes garbage?[18] Do we accept being pressed on every side, perplexed, persecuted, and struck down?[19] Do we accept that the path to delight and worship passes through every single IT in our lives? Since no human has ever found the key to unlock the answers for suffering, do we allow others time and space to wrestle with it?

God promises His understanding and presence in the face of suffering. He can and does intervene with miracles, but do we graciously accept that He often answers by telling us to wait or even saying *no*? What if He calls us to walk only in the fellowship of His sufferings and not in the glory of success? Faithful Christian wives and mothers struggle to keep their sanity while being caregivers to husbands with Alzheimer's disease and children with autism. Pornography travels at lightning speed on social media, increasing sexual abuse and incest even in our churches. Missionaries suffer for their prodigal children who bitterly turn their backs on God. Domestic violence and church divisions add to a growing cynicism of helplessness and hopelessness. Not even Scripture avoids unpleasant, at times horrific, experiences.

Joseph, betrayed by his brothers, cried frequently and often audibly. Job not only endured great loss but also superficial answers from his friends. Psalm 126:5–6 serves as a container for the tears of sowing. The writer of Psalm 88 had the courage to end his song in a minor key of grief instead of praise like the other hundred and forty-nine psalms. Isaiah 50:10 doesn't ignore the walk in the dark. Jeremiah, the crying prophet, wrote Lamentations. Acts 12 records that God released Peter from prison but allowed Herod to kill James. Paul wasn't healed,[20] and he left Trophimus sick.[21] Hebrews 11:36–40 includes the stories of those who didn't escape torture and pain. Did these followers of God somehow come up short in their faith and prayers? Was there unconfessed sin in their lives? Did they get punished for their fathers' sins, or was God disciplining them? Were they simply walking through the reality of life?

Andrew Fellows maintains that, as Christians walk through the reality of suffering and the resulting tension, deep lamentations are a gift from God. True lamenting is a gut-wrenching plea for God to be who He is and do what He has promised for the very sake of His name. It is calling God into a situation that makes no sense. It is working through paradoxes with both head and heart, accepting that many times reality is painful. Mr. Fellows believes that lamenting is not a lack of faith but a way to avoid superficial worship.[22] Some worship services center exclusively on praise songs that help everyone feel good. That choice could create guilt and shame in those who hide their struggles behind forced smiles. If you were invited

---

[18] Philippians 3:8–11.

[19] 2 Corinthians 4:8.

[20] 2 Corinthians 12:7–10.

[21] 2 Timothy 4:20.

[22] Andrew Fellows, "A Time to Grieve: A Lamentation for the Loss of Lament" (workshop presented at the annual meeting of the European Leadership Forum, Wisla, Poland, May 30–June 4, 2015).

to sit silently in the presence of trauma victims or the grieving, would you put on your coat and hurry out the door? Or would you sit quietly in the IT area and truly worship the resurrected and scarred Christ? The creative clusters endeavor to provide this time and space for lamenting. It is represented symbolically by the space between God's names and Satan's territory of antonyms. The more energy we invest in running toward suffering, the more passion we will free up to minister to one another in love.

Push Back

Once you have identified the issues in your invisible tension area, you can start pushing back against the IT with God's help, as stated in Isaiah 28:6b, "He will be ... a source of strength to those who turn back the battle at the gate." Hezekiah assembled his military officers at the city gate and encouraged them, saying, "There is a greater power with us than with him."[23] David ran toward his enemies by embracing his responsibilities as a well-equipped soldier, but he depended solely on God's power. He would often mention this teamwork by stating, "In the name of the Lord, I cut them off." When do we stand firm at the gate, and when do we march out into battle? How much will God do for us, and how much are we to do for Him? While that balance can be difficult to discern at times, we can be certain that He wants us fully equipped, positioned at the gate, and ready to push back as He leads.[24]

The "Push back" area offers three key Bible verses that interlock with God's names, the seeds, and the practical application verses of each map. There are hundreds of other verses that could be substituted in this area. The choice of these verses can be flexible, depending on the Holy Spirit's guidance during personal devotions and Bible study. It is essential to use Scripture to push back against Satan. Jesus set an example for us when He was tempted by Satan and drew His sword.[25] It wasn't the time to debate with the enemy. Since it was essential for Jesus to battle in this way, we can be certain that anything less on our part will weaken our effort to turn back the battle at the gate. We may find ourselves praying more before and after problems instead of during them. If that is true, maybe we overestimate our strength and underestimate the power of praying God's Word and His names. Prayer thwarts Satan's tactics as God transforms pain and suffering into His glory and our good.[26] It takes great perseverance to push back the battle at the gate while waiting for our heads and hearts to harmonize.

---

[23] 2 Chronicles 32:6–8.
[24] Ephesians 6:10–18.
[25] Matthew 4:1-11; Hebrews 4:12.
[26] Romans 5:3–5.

Integration

A synonym for *integration* is *amalgamation*. An amalgam is a combination of two or more unlike things into one.[27] A oneness or wholeness of spirit can be reached only by combining the tension of the head and heart. This process proves challenging under normal circumstances and becomes titanic in the face of trauma and loss. My personal journey of healing was hindered by well-intentioned Christians who only reasoned with my head. Their certainty of direction reassured me, but their logical conclusions about God and how I should respond to Him became legalistic in nature. What they missed was that my heart was broken, not my head. Our relationships became strained by growing mistrust. On the other hand, my counseling associates offered me an unlimited supply of warm acceptance. They fed my expectations that deeper introspection could somehow free me and encouraged me to follow my heart. These relationships eventually became too enmeshed. No matter which way I turned, I couldn't find the path to wholeness. It was difficult for me to accept the past, live in the present, and hope for the future.

Paul Tournier addressed the opposing forces of revolt and acceptance in which I found myself stranded. To insist that someone be courageous and accept what has happened to him doesn't allow for the laborious elaboration of injustices or adversities. Acceptance is not so much a concept to encourage as an attitude to transmit. Those who have slowly learned to accept their difficulties can influence others who suffer. Their integration of empathy, love, and truth with their own struggles creates what Dr. Tournier calls "spiritual contact, communion, genuine encounter, the flash, reciprocity."[28] God sent several authentic helpers who showed me the way out from the disintegration of trauma. Our genuine encounters will never be forgotten. One of these special helpers still creates frequent flashes for me and those around him.

His story started many years ago in a small, rural town near Indianapolis. He grew up in a beautiful, historic tollhouse dedicated to road maintenance for travelers. It is symbolic that his childhood home still stands as a protected landmark while he lives halfway around the world. His desire to explore unknown territory started at a young age. His Sunday school teacher had just finished a lesson about one of Paul's missionary journeys when he raised his hand and said, "Mrs. Brooks, I want to be a missionary just like Paul." He was only nine years old. Three years later God arranged for him to attend a Christian camp. There he met a young girl. They laughed and played for hours in the swimming pool and quickly became best friends. Seven years later, in a different swimming pool, their laughter and play turned into tears and trauma.

On August 1, 1969, the young man said, "This will be my last dive for the night." For whatever reason, he pushed off too hard and hit his head on the bottom of the pool, fracturing his neck. Her parents immediately pressured her to break off the engagement. His parents

---

[27] http://www.vocabulary.com, accessed December 2, 2016.

[28] Paul Tournier, *A Listening Ear: Reflections on Christian Caring* (Minneapolis: Augsburg Publishing House, 1987), 33–37.

strongly advised him to reconsider his career choice. Did the angels in heaven hold their breath while waiting to see the epilogue?

Epilogue

The Lion of Judah stepped forward, tossed a ball to the young man, and said, "Do you love me more than these? Feed my sheep." Though broken, he became a missionary, just like Paul. Although he has asked repeatedly to be healed, just like Paul, the thorn in his flesh never leaves him. He is a housebound prisoner in Italy, just like Paul. Also just like Paul, he daily accepts God's truth that "grace is sufficient … for My power is made perfect in weakness."[29] No matter how much the beast of suffering invades his cage, he never lets it define him as a person. Our daughter captured the intensity of my husband's battle and the tenacity of his faith in the following poem, "Graceful Lament."

Three lions are before you. Three lions toss balls. The first lion is the lion of suffering. Whether physically, mentally, emotionally, or spiritually, he will try to deform you and discourage you from making the journey back home. He appears when least expected and stays much longer than wanted. By God's grace, we are to lament and accept the presence of this lion but not what he throws. The second lion is the roaring lion. He prowls around looking for someone to deceive, blame, and shame.[30] He will try to convince you that your resistance is useless and that you should despair. He despises worship, prayer, and God's names. Our old man knows him all too well—our new man stands firm against him. The third Lion roared from the cross, "It is finished." By means of His death and resurrection, He is the only one worthy to open the scroll and the seven seals in heaven.[31] The Lion of Judah invites us to journey to His Father's heart where we will find the Lamb who overcomes. Like Lucy in the epilogue of *Narnia*, we are told to keep our eyes open. Will we see and persevere on His path of delightful grace, or will we allow the other two lions to devour us?

---

[29] 2 Corinthians 12:9.
[30] 1 Peter 5:8.
[31] Revelation 5:5–6.

Graceful Lament

by Stephany Wolsieffer Bruno

A villanelle to my father, Jim, for his courage and perseverance in the face of suffering.

Martyr, the lion rent your neck with fierce rage.
You lifted your eyes to Heaven and offered God your humble praise.
Martyr, from that day, the lion chose to use your body as his cage.

Next your arms, your hands, your legs. The lion roared: "The wage
Of your faithfulness is pain. Do you still want to follow His ways?"
Martyr, the lion rent your neck with fierce rage.

No pause, no rest, no break from daily carnage;
"Send an angel to stop his mouth," your little girls pray.
Martyr, the lion chose to use your body as a cage.

Even when the lion sleeps, your body remains a cage.
"Just give him the strength to wrestle," your little girls pray.
Martyr, the lion rent your neck with fierce rage.

Now he chews at your muscles, your nerves, your mind he tries to disengage.
Tamed? Never, not him, not you.
Martyr, the lion chose to use your body as a cage.

Beginning at a very early age
This became your lot, your witness, your life:
Martyrdom until the end of your days.

The lion rent your neck with fierce rage
And from that day he chose to use your body as his cage.

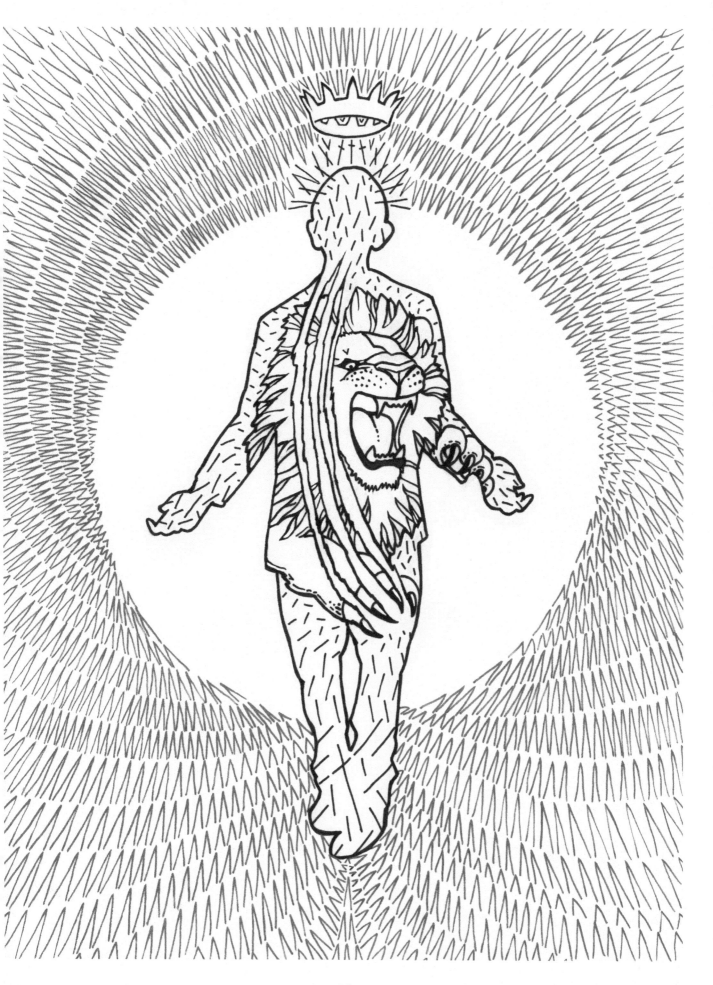

Section 2

For the Sake of His Name

Jesus said to them,

I tell you the truth,

Before Abraham was born,

I AM.

John 8:58

Five Clusters for the Sake of His Name

1. **Awesome, Glorious, Majestic Name**
2. **Everlasting Name**
3. **Good and Only Name**
4. **Great and Powerful Name**
5. **Holy Name**

These five clusters combine biblical descriptions of God's names with the privileges and responsibilities to love and live His names. At the top of each cluster, there are descriptions of His names. At the bottom of each cluster is the foundation of the frequent biblical expression "for the sake of His name." Unfolding from bottom to top are the various privileges and responsibilities. Selecting and grouping the privileges and responsibilities with the descriptions of God's names takes prayer, meditation, and worship. You could take the same descriptions, privileges, and responsibilities and create your own clusters, either smaller or larger. There is no right or wrong way to do it. It is not so much about the final product as about deepening your relationship with God while clustering.

"Describe His Names" is an alphabetical list of nine descriptions of God's names with a brief Scripture index. These few Scriptures, among the many in the Bible, draw our minds and hearts close to His personal presence and yet remind us to respect His awesome otherness. He is our friend, and we are invited to walk by His side, and yet we are to remember that there is no one like Him as He sits on His throne. We often read in the Bible that those who found themselves in God's immediate presence fell on their faces. Jewish tradition teaches that scribes had to wipe their writing tools and bathe their entire bodies before writing *Jehovah*. While we don't want to lose sight of God as loving Father, is it possible that, at times, we forget that He is also the Most High? Clustering the descriptions of His names can help us maintain a godly balance between intimacy and reverent awe (fear) in our prayers, meditations, and worship.

"Love and Live His Names" is an alphabetical list with a brief Scripture index of our privileges and responsibilities. Walking in His presence should change how we walk in family, church, and social life. God, Jesus Christ, and the Holy Spirit reveal themselves in Their names and call each one of us by name to respond and act accordingly. This is not a passive relationship that we enter into when it is convenient and walk away from when the going gets rough. He invites us into a dynamic relationship and asks us to make every effort to be transformed in our thinking and behavior while He transforms us in our very being. Out of approximately fifty privileges and responsibilities, only five commands indicate what we are not to do with His name. May we truly grasp why God gave us those five commandments and gasp out loud when someone takes His name in vain! From the burning bush to Christ on earth, the great I AM THAT I AM speaks to us. We truly stand on holy ground.

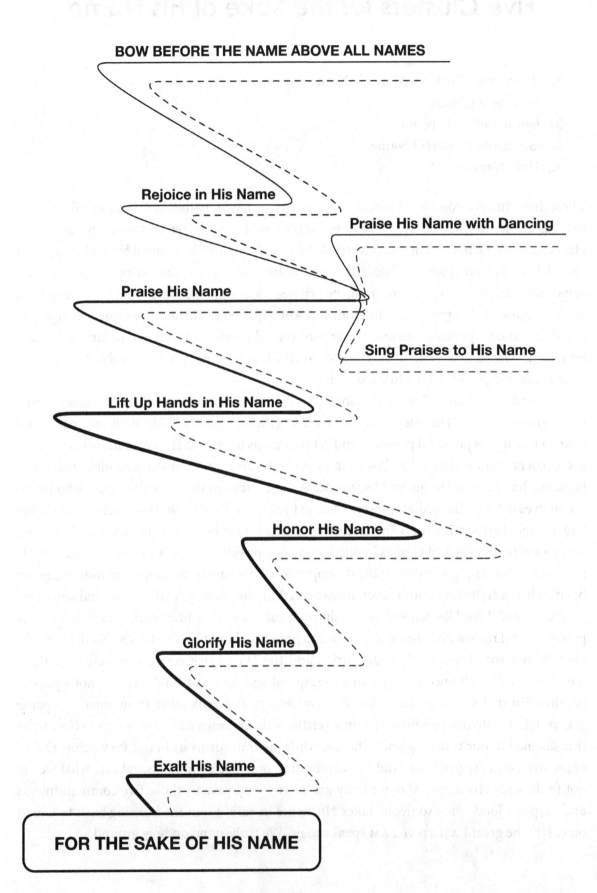

AWESOME, GLORIOUS, MAJESTIC NAME

BOW BEFORE THE NAME ABOVE ALL NAMES

Rejoice in His Name

Praise His Name with Dancing

Praise His Name

Sing Praises to His Name

Lift Up Hands in His Name

Honor His Name

Glorify His Name

Exalt His Name

FOR THE SAKE OF HIS NAME

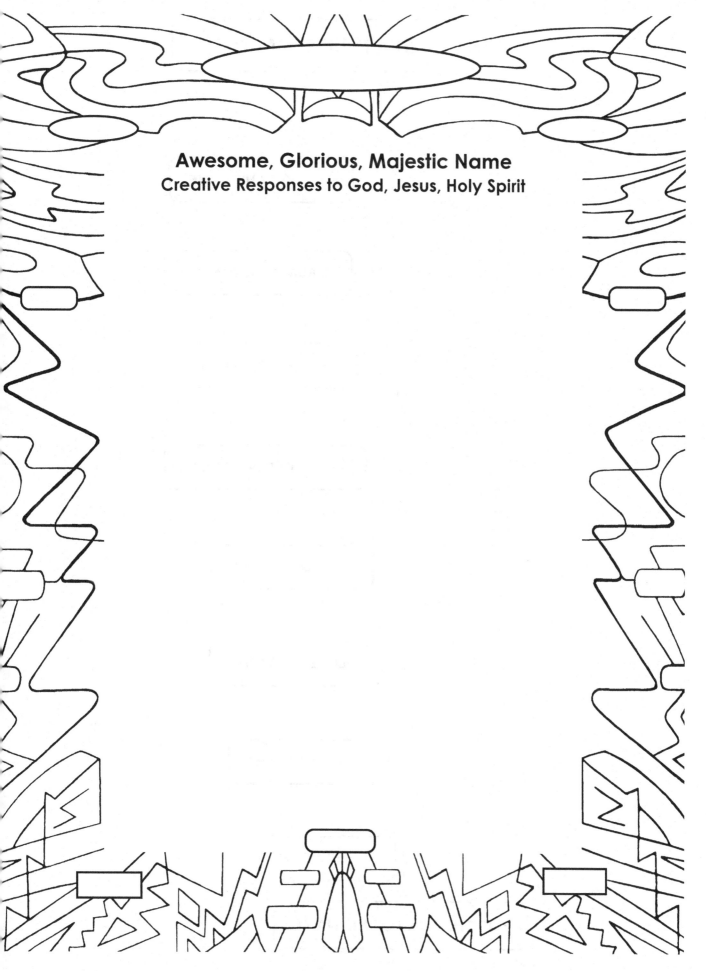

Awesome, Glorious, Majestic Name
Creative Responses to God, Jesus, Holy Spirit

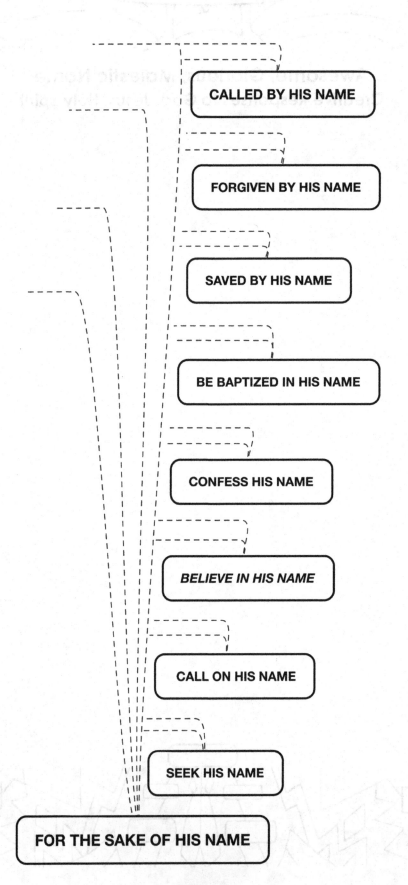

EVERLASTING NAME

CALLED BY HIS NAME

FORGIVEN BY HIS NAME

SAVED BY HIS NAME

BE BAPTIZED IN HIS NAME

CONFESS HIS NAME

BELIEVE IN HIS NAME

CALL ON HIS NAME

SEEK HIS NAME

FOR THE SAKE OF HIS NAME

Everlasting Name
Creative Responses to God, Jesus, Holy Spirit

GOOD AND ONLY NAME

SERVE IN HIS NAME

ANOINT WITH OIL IN HIS NAME

PERFORM MIRACLES IN HIS NAME

GATHER TOGETHER IN HIS NAME

BUILD A PLACE FOR HIS NAME

BLESSED WHO COMES IN HIS NAME

BLESS IN HIS NAME

BLESS HIS NAME

REMEMBER HIS NAME

FOR THE SAKE OF HIS NAME

Good and Only Name
Creative Responses to God, Jesus, Holy Spirit

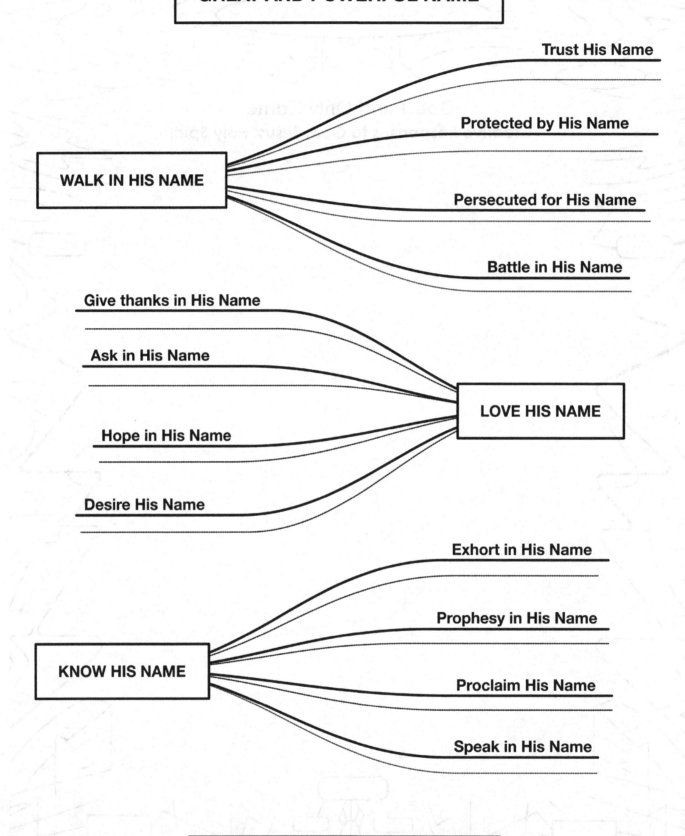

GREAT AND POWERFUL NAME

Trust His Name

Protected by His Name

WALK IN HIS NAME

Persecuted for His Name

Battle in His Name

Give thanks in His Name

Ask in His Name

LOVE HIS NAME

Hope in His Name

Desire His Name

Exhort in His Name

Prophesy in His Name

KNOW HIS NAME

Proclaim His Name

Speak in His Name

FOR THE SAKE OF HIS NAME

Great and Powerful Name

Creative Responses to God, Jesus, Holy Spirit

HOLY NAME

Delight to Fear in His Name — DO NOT deny His Name

Fear His Name — DO NOT prophesy falsely in His Name

Take oaths in His Name — DO NOT swear falsely by His Name

Sanctify His Name — DO NOT blasphemy His Name

Reverence His Name — DO NOT misuse His Name

FOR THE SAKE OF HIS NAME

Holy Name
Creative Responses to God, Jesus, Holy Spirit

Describe His Names

Scripture Index (NIV, NASB, KJV)

Awesome name
(Deuteronomy 28:58; Psalms 99:3, 111:9)

Everlasting (enduring) name
(Exodus 3:15; Nehemiah 9:10; Psalms 72:17, 135:13; Isaiah 63:12, 63:16; Daniel 9:15)

Glorious name (glory to)
(Deuteronomy 28:58; 1 Chronicles 29:13; Nehemiah 9:5; Psalms 66:2, 72:19, 79:9, 96:8, and 115:1; Isaiah 63:14)

Good (fair, noble) name
(Psalms 52:9, 54:6; James 2:7)

Great name
(Joshua 7:9; 1 Samuel 12:22; 1 Kings 8:42; 1 Chronicles 17:24; 2 Chronicles 6:32; Psalms 76:1, 99:3; Jeremiah 44:26; Ezekiel 36:23; Malachi 1:11)

Holy name
(1 Chronicles 16:10, 16:35; Psalms 30:4, 97:12, 103:1, 105:3, 106:47, and 111:9; Isaiah 29:23, 57:15; Ezekiel 20:39, 36:20–23, 39:7, 39:25, and 43:7–8; Amos 2:7; Luke 1:49)

Majestic (superior) name
(Psalm 8:1, 8:9; Micah 5:4; Hebrews 1:4)

Only name (no other God)
(Deuteronomy 6:4; Isaiah 45:21–22; Zechariah 14:9; Romans 16:27; Ephesians 4:4–6; Jude 1:25)

Powerful (proclaimed, well-known) name
(Exodus 9:16; Jeremiah 10:6, 32:18–19; Mark 6:14; John 17:11–12; Revelation 5:13, 19:1)

Love and Live His Names

Scripture Index (NIV, NASB, KJV)

Anoint with oil in His name (James 5:14)

Ask in His name (Matthew 7:7; John 14:13–14, 15:16, and 16:23–27)

Baptize (be baptized) in His name (Matthew 28:19; Acts 2:38, 8:12, 8:16, 10:48, 19:5, and 22:16)

Battle in His name (1 Samuel 17:45; 2 Chronicles 14:11; Psalms 20:5, 44:5, 89:19–29, and 118:10–14; Isaiah 30:27, 64:2; Revelation 2:13)

Believe (have faith) in His name (John 1:12, 2:23, and 20:31; Acts 3:16; 1 John 3:23, 5:13)

Bless His name (Genesis 9:26, 14:20; Nehemiah 9:5; John 12:13; 1 Timothy 1:11, 6:15)

Bless in His name (Genesis 48:15–16; Numbers 6:22–27; Deuteronomy 10:8, 21:5; Ruth 2:4; 2 Samuel 6:18; 1 Kings 8:14, 8:55; 1 Chronicles 16:2, 23:13; Mark 10:16)

Blessed who comes in His name (Psalm 118:26; Matthew 21:9, 23:39; Mark 11:9; Luke 13:35, 19:38; John 12:13)

Bow before the name above all names (Philippians 2:9–11)

Build a place for His name (Deuteronomy 12:5, 12:11, 14:23–24, 16:2, 16:6, 16:11, and 26:2; 2 Samuel 7:13; 1 Kings 5:3, 5:5, 8:16–20, 8:29, 8:43–48, and 9:3; 1 Chronicles 22:19, 29:16; 2 Chronicles 2:1, 2:4, 6:5–10, 7:16, and 20:8–9)

Call on His name (Genesis 4:26, 12:8, 13:4, 21:33, and 26:25; 1 Kings 18:24; 1 Chronicles 16:8; Psalms 50:15, 80:18, 99:6, 105:1, 116:4, 116:13, and 116:17; Isaiah 12:4; Lamentations 3:55; Joel 2:32; Zephaniah 3:9; Zechariah 13:9; Acts 2:21, 22:16; Romans 10:13; 1 Corinthians 1:2)

Called by His name (people) (Deuteronomy 28:10; 2 Chronicles 7:14; Isaiah 43:7; Jeremiah 14:9, 15:16; Daniel 9:19; Acts 15:17; Ephesians 3:15; 1 Peter 4:16; Revelation 3:12, 14:1, and 22:4)

Called by His name (place) (1 Kings 11:36, 14:21; 2 Chronicles 12:13, 33:4, and 33:7; Nehemiah 1:9; Psalm 74:7; Isaiah 18:7; Jeremiah 7:10–14, 25:29, 32:34, and 34:15; Ezekiel 48:35; Daniel 9:18–19; Revelation 3:12)

Confess His name (1 Kings 8:33, 8:35; 2 Chronicles 6:24–26; 2 Timothy 2:19; Hebrews 13:15)

Delight to fear His name (Nehemiah 1:11)

Desire His name (Isaiah 26:8)

Do not blaspheme (slander, curse) His name (Leviticus 24:11–16; Romans 2:23–24; 1 Timothy 6:1; James 2:5–7; Revelation 13:6, 16:9)

Do not deny His name (Luke 22:34, 22:54–62; 2 Peter 2:1; Jude 1:4; Revelation 3:8)

Do not misuse (show contempt, profane, defile, revile) His name (Exodus 20:7; Leviticus 18:21, 20:3, 21:6, 22:2, and 22:32; Deuteronomy 5:11; Psalms 74:7, 74:10, 74:18, and 139:20; Proverbs 30:9; Jeremiah 34:16; Ezekiel 20:39, 36:20–23, 39:7, and 43:7–8; Amos 2:7; Malachi 1:6–8)

Do not prophesy falsely (lie, deceive) in His name (Jeremiah 27:15, 29:9, 29:21, and 29:23; Zechariah 13:2–3; Matthew 7:21–23, 24:5; Mark 13:6; Luke 21:8; Acts 19:13–16)

Do not swear falsely by His name (Leviticus 19:12; Zechariah 5:3–4; Matthew 5:33–37, 23:16–22)

Exalt (magnify, give high honor to) His name (2 Samuel 7:22–26; 1 Chronicles 17:23–24; Nehemiah 9:5–6; Psalms 34:3, 138:2, 145:2, and 148:13; Isaiah 12:4, 24:15; Acts 19:17)

Exhort in His name (1 Corinthians 1:10, 5:3–5; 2 Thessalonians 3:6)

Fear His name (1 Kings 8:43; 2 Chronicles 6:33; Psalms 61:5, 86:11, and 102:15; Isaiah 59:19; Micah 6:9; Malachi 1:14, 4:2; Acts 19:17; Revelation 11:18)

Forgiven by His Name (Psalm 79:9; Luke 24:47; Acts 2:38, 10:43, and 22:16; 1 John 2:12)

Gather together in His name (Matthew 18:20; 1 Corinthians 5:4)

Give thanks to (in) His name (1 Chronicles 16:35; Psalms 75:1, 106:47; Ephesians 5:20)

Glorify (glory in) His name (1 Chronicles 16:10, 16:29; Psalms 29:2, 86:9, 86:12, 96:8, 105:3, and 115:1; Isaiah 24:15; John 12:28; 2 Thessalonians 1:12; Revelation 15:3–4)

Honor (awe, esteem) His name (Exodus 20:24; Isaiah 26:13; Jeremiah 3:17; Malachi 2:2, 2:5, and 3:16; Acts 19:17)

Hope in His name (Psalm 52:9; Matthew 12:21)

Know (acknowledge) His name (2 Chronicles 6:33; Psalms 9:10, 83:18, and 91:14; Isaiah 52:6; Jeremiah 16:21)

Lift up hands in His name (Psalm 63:4)

Love His name (Psalms 5:11, 69:36, and 119:132; Isaiah 56:6)

Perform miracles in His name (Mark 9:38–39, 16:17–18; Luke 9:49–50, 10:17; John 10:25; Acts 3:6, 3:16, 4:10, 4:30, and 16:18)

Persecuted (hated, shamed) for His name (Matthew 10:22, 24:9; Mark 13:13; Luke 21:12–19; John 15:20–21; Acts 4:17–20, 5:28, 5:33, 5:40–41, 9:14, 9:16, 15:26, 21:13, and 26:9–10; 1 Peter 4:14; Revelation 2:3)

Praise His name (1 Chronicles 29:13; Job 1:21; Psalms 30:4, 44:8, 54:6, 69:30, 72:19, 74:21, 97:12, 99:3, 100:4, 103:1, 113:1–3, 122:4, 135:1, 138:2, 140:13, 142:7, 145:1, 145:21, 148:5, and 148:13; Isaiah 25:1; Joel 2:26)

Praise His name with dancing (Exodus 15:20–21; 2 Samuel 6:14–15; Psalms 30:11–12, 149:3, and 150:4; Jeremiah 31:12–14)

Proclaim (declare, preach) His Name (Exodus 9:16; Deuteronomy 32:3; Psalms 22:22, 102:21; Isaiah 12:4; Luke 24:47; Acts 8:12, 9:27–28; Romans 9:17; Hebrews 2:12)

Prophesy in His name (Ezra 5:1; Jeremiah 26:9; Daniel 9:6; James 5:10)

Protected by His name (Psalms 5:11, 20:1, and 91:14; John 17:11–12)

Rejoice (delight) in His name (Nehemiah 1:11; Psalms 5:11, 89:16; Romans 5:11)

Remember His name (Nehemiah 4:14; Psalms 63:6–8, 78:35, and 119:55; 2 Timothy 2:8)

Revere His name (Deuteronomy 28:58; Malachi 4:2; Revelation 11:18)

Sanctify (hallow, keep holy) His name (Isaiah 29:23; Matthew 6:9; Luke 11:2)

Saved (helped, protected, justified, sanctified, washed) by His name (Psalms 20:1, 54:1, and 124:8; Joel 2:32; Matthew 1:21; John 17:11–12; Acts 2:21, 4:12; Romans 10:13; 1 Corinthians 6:11)

Seek His name (Psalm 83:16; Matthew 7:7–8; Hebrews 11:6)

Serve (welcome) in His name (Deuteronomy 18:5–7, 21:5; Matthew 18:5; Mark 9:37; Luke 9:48; Colossians 3:17; 1 Timothy 6:1)

Sing praises to His name (2 Samuel 22:50; Psalms 7:17, 9:2, 18:49, 61:8, 66:2, 66:4, 68:4, 69:30, 89:12, 92:1, and 135:3; Romans 15:9; Colossians 3:16–17)

Speak in His name (Exodus 5:23; Deuteronomy 18:18–19)

Take oaths in His name (Deuteronomy 6:13, 10:20; 1 Samuel 20:42; Nehemiah 13:25; Psalm 63:11; Isaiah 48:1; Jeremiah 12:16, 44:26)

Trust (take refuge) in His name (Psalms 9:10; 20:7, and 33:21; Proverbs 18:10; Isaiah 50:10; Zephaniah 3:12)

Walk in His name (Micah 4:5; Zechariah 10:12; Acts 3:6)

Section 3

Creative Clusters

On his robe and on his thigh he has this name written:

KING OF KINGS AND LORD OF LORDS.

Revelation 19:16

CHAPTER 1

Awesome God: Deity

List of Creative Clusters

Ageless Splendor

Be Still and Know

Fragrance of Life

In the Beginning

Set Apart by Design

Your Will Be Done

Carrie's Joy: Found

(awe)

Carrie found an extraordinary butterfly in a very unusual place. She rescued her, took her home, and named her Joy. Concerned for Joy's safety, she pulled out the family's old, abandoned aquarium and created a beautiful butterfly haven. Carrie loved caring for Joy, and Joy loved being with Carrie. Staying close to one another kept the lonely darkness far away.[32]

---

[32] The story of Carrie's butterfly, Joy, is based on a true story of a little boy, his ladybug, and a special box.

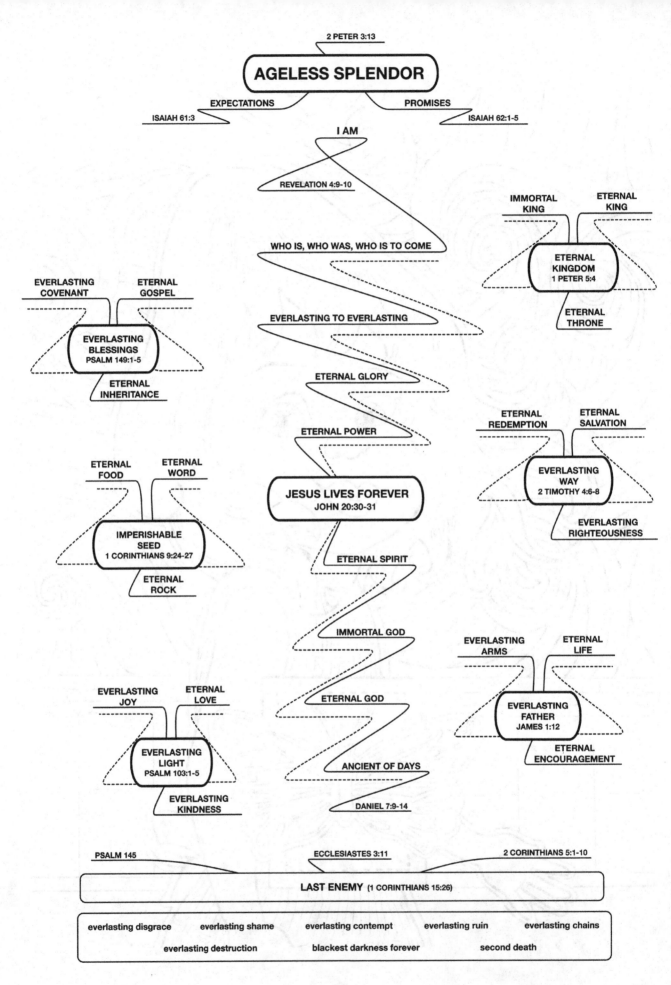

2 PETER 3:13

AGELESS SPLENDOR

EXPECTATIONS   PROMISES

ISAIAH 61:3   ISAIAH 62:1-5

I AM

REVELATION 4:9-10

IMMORTAL KING   ETERNAL KING

WHO IS, WHO WAS, WHO IS TO COME

ETERNAL KINGDOM
1 PETER 5:4

EVERLASTING COVENANT   ETERNAL GOSPEL

ETERNAL THRONE

EVERLASTING TO EVERLASTING

EVERLASTING BLESSINGS
PSALM 149:1-5

ETERNAL INHERITANCE

ETERNAL GLORY

ETERNAL POWER

ETERNAL REDEMPTION   ETERNAL SALVATION

ETERNAL FOOD   ETERNAL WORD

EVERLASTING WAY
2 TIMOTHY 4:6-8

JESUS LIVES FOREVER
JOHN 20:30-31

EVERLASTING RIGHTEOUSNESS

IMPERISHABLE SEED
1 CORINTHIANS 9:24-27

ETERNAL ROCK

ETERNAL SPIRIT

IMMORTAL GOD

EVERLASTING ARMS   ETERNAL LIFE

EVERLASTING JOY   ETERNAL LOVE

ETERNAL GOD

EVERLASTING FATHER
JAMES 1:12

EVERLASTING LIGHT
PSALM 103:1-5

ETERNAL ENCOURAGEMENT

EVERLASTING KINDNESS

ANCIENT OF DAYS

DANIEL 7:9-14

PSALM 145   ECCLESIASTES 3:11   2 CORINTHIANS 5:1-10

LAST ENEMY (1 CORINTHIANS 15:26)

everlasting disgrace   everlasting shame   everlasting contempt   everlasting ruin   everlasting chains

everlasting destruction   blackest darkness forever   second death

Ageless Splendor
Creative Responses to God, Jesus, Holy Spirit

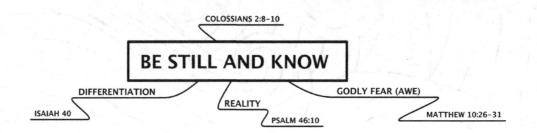

BE STILL AND KNOW

COLOSSIANS 2:8-10

DIFFERENTIATION

ISAIAH 40

REALITY

PSALM 46:10

GODLY FEAR (AWE)

MATTHEW 10:26-31

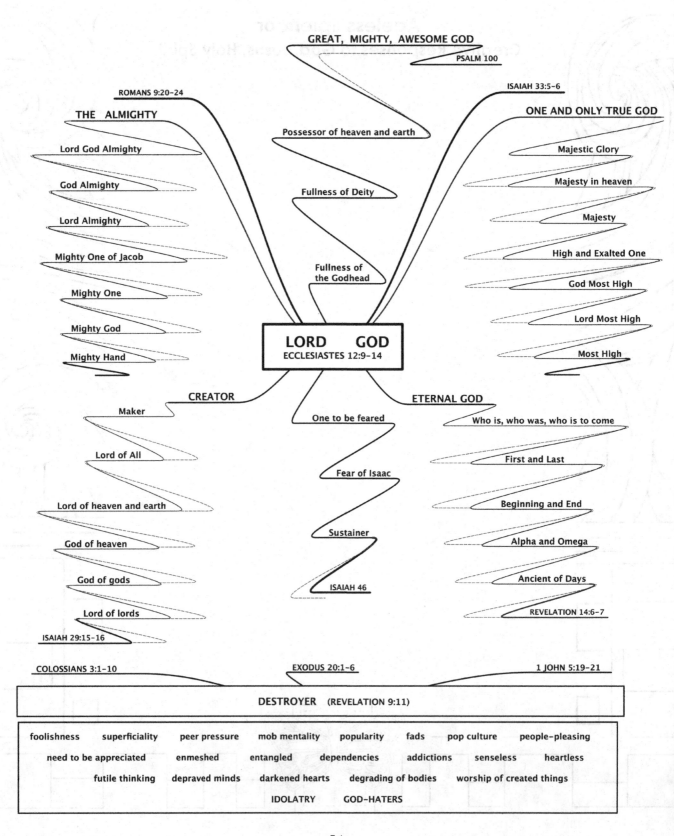

GREAT, MIGHTY, AWESOME GOD

PSALM 100

ROMANS 9:20-24

ISAIAH 33:5-6

THE ALMIGHTY

Lord God Almighty

God Almighty

Lord Almighty

Mighty One of Jacob

Mighty One

Mighty God

Mighty Hand

Possessor of heaven and earth

Fullness of Deity

Fullness of
the Godhead

ONE AND ONLY TRUE GOD

Majestic Glory

Majesty in heaven

Majesty

High and Exalted One

God Most High

Lord Most High

Most High

LORD   GOD
ECCLESIASTES 12:9-14

CREATOR

Maker

Lord of All

Lord of heaven and earth

God of heaven

God of gods

Lord of lords

ISAIAH 29:15-16

One to be feared

Fear of Isaac

Sustainer

ISAIAH 46

ETERNAL GOD

Who is, who was, who is to come

First and Last

Beginning and End

Alpha and Omega

Ancient of Days

REVELATION 14:6-7

COLOSSIANS 3:1-10

EXODUS 20:1-6

1 JOHN 5:19-21

DESTROYER   (REVELATION 9:11)

| foolishness | superficiality | peer pressure | mob mentality | popularity | fads | pop culture | people-pleasing |

need to be appreciated   enmeshed   entangled   dependencies   addictions   senseless   heartless

futile thinking   depraved minds   darkened hearts   degrading of bodies   worship of created things

IDOLATRY   GOD-HATERS

Be Still and Know
Creative Responses to God, Jesus, Holy Spirit

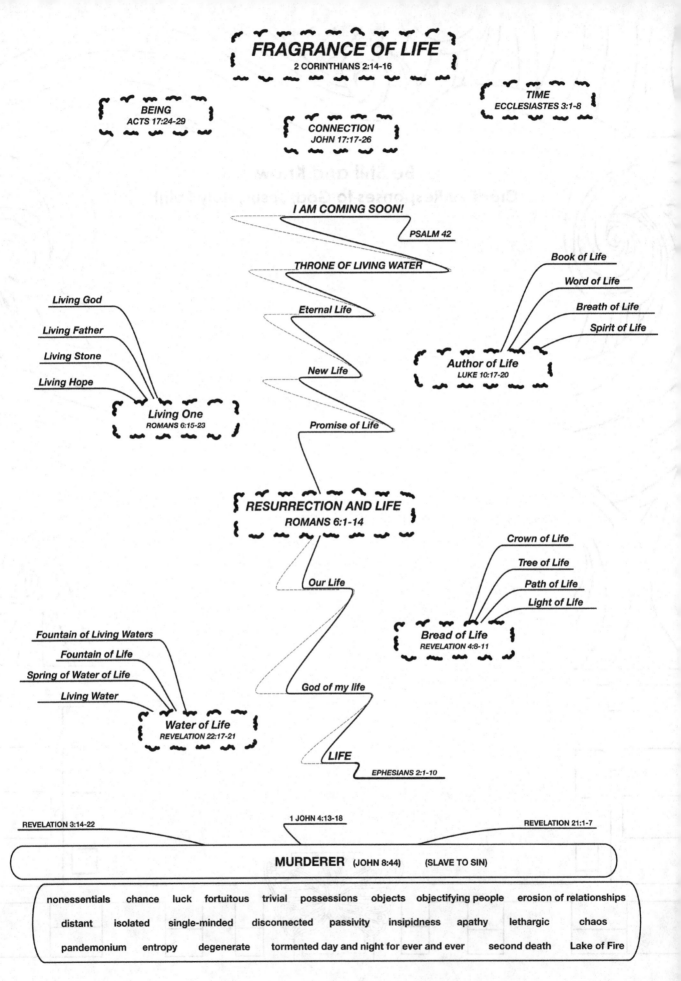

FRAGRANCE OF LIFE
2 CORINTHIANS 2:14-16

BEING
ACTS 17:24-29

CONNECTION
JOHN 17:17-26

TIME
ECCLESIASTES 3:1-8

I AM COMING SOON!

PSALM 42

THRONE OF LIVING WATER

Eternal Life

Book of Life

Word of Life

Breath of Life

Spirit of Life

Living God

Living Father

Living Stone

Living Hope

New Life

Author of Life
LUKE 10:17-20

Living One
ROMANS 6:15-23

Promise of Life

RESURRECTION AND LIFE
ROMANS 6:1-14

Crown of Life

Tree of Life

Path of Life

Light of Life

Our Life

Bread of Life
REVELATION 4:8-11

Fountain of Living Waters

Fountain of Life

Spring of Water of Life

Living Water

God of my life

Water of Life
REVELATION 22:17-21

LIFE

EPHESIANS 2:1-10

REVELATION 3:14-22

1 JOHN 4:13-18

REVELATION 21:1-7

MURDERER (JOHN 8:44)   (SLAVE TO SIN)

nonessentials   chance   luck   fortuitous   trivial   possessions   objects   objectifying people   erosion of relationships

distant   isolated   single-minded   disconnected   passivity   insipidness   apathy   lethargic   chaos

pandemonium   entropy   degenerate   tormented day and night for ever and ever   second death   Lake of Fire

Fragrance of Life
Creative Responses to God, Jesus, Holy Spirit

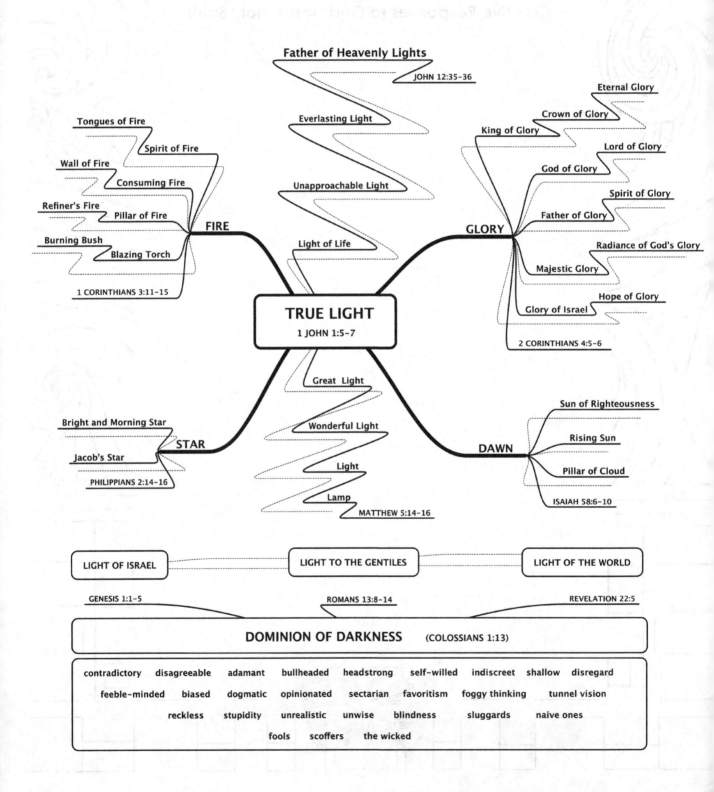

EPHESIANS 5:8-17

IN THE BEGINNING

KNOWLEDGE — WISDOM — UNDERSTANDING

COLOSSIANS 1:9-14

DANIEL 12:1-3

PROVERBS 4:1-9

Father of Heavenly Lights

JOHN 12:35-36

Everlasting Light

Unapproachable Light

Light of Life

FIRE

Tongues of Fire
Spirit of Fire
Wall of Fire
Consuming Fire
Refiner's Fire
Pillar of Fire
Burning Bush
Blazing Torch

1 CORINTHIANS 3:11-15

GLORY

Eternal Glory
Crown of Glory
King of Glory
Lord of Glory
God of Glory
Spirit of Glory
Father of Glory
Radiance of God's Glory
Majestic Glory
Hope of Glory
Glory of Israel

2 CORINTHIANS 4:5-6

TRUE LIGHT
1 JOHN 1:5-7

Great Light

Wonderful Light

Light

Lamp

MATTHEW 5:14-16

STAR

Bright and Morning Star
Jacob's Star

PHILIPPIANS 2:14-16

DAWN

Sun of Righteousness
Rising Sun
Pillar of Cloud

ISAIAH 58:6-10

LIGHT OF ISRAEL — LIGHT TO THE GENTILES — LIGHT OF THE WORLD

GENESIS 1:1-5

ROMANS 13:8-14

REVELATION 22:5

DOMINION OF DARKNESS   (COLOSSIANS 1:13)

contradictory   disagreeable   adamant   bullheaded   headstrong   self-willed   indiscreet   shallow   disregard

feeble-minded   biased   dogmatic   opinionated   sectarian   favoritism   foggy thinking   tunnel vision

reckless   stupidity   unrealistic   unwise   blindness   sluggards   naive ones

fools   scoffers   the wicked

In the Beginning
Creative Responses to God, Jesus, Holy Spirit

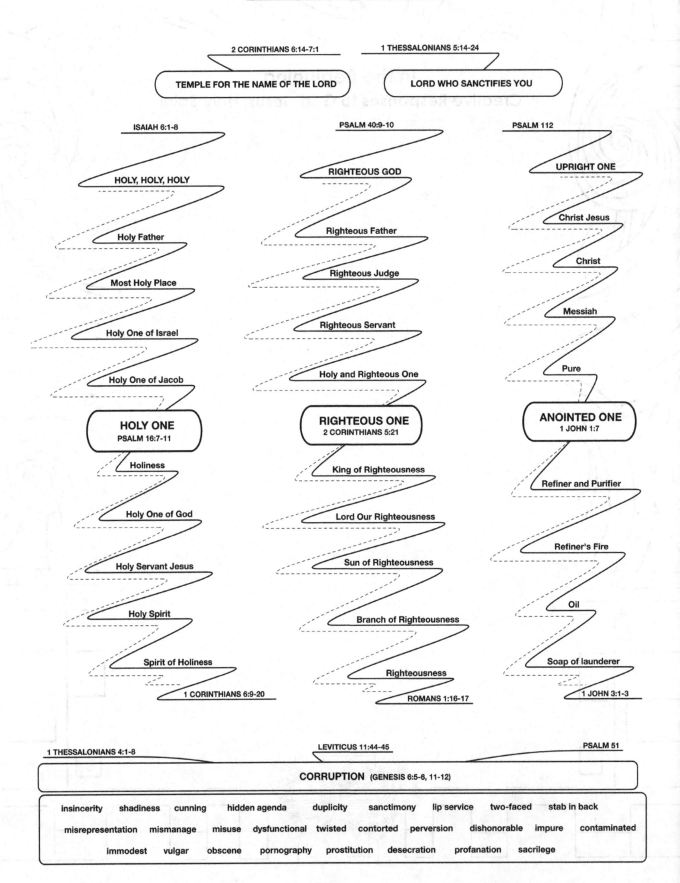

GODLINESS
2 PETER 3:11-14

SET APART BY DESIGN
2 THESSALONIANS 2:13-17

AUTHENTICITY
PHILIPPIANS 2:14-18

2 CORINTHIANS 6:14-7:1

TEMPLE FOR THE NAME OF THE LORD

1 THESSALONIANS 5:14-24

LORD WHO SANCTIFIES YOU

ISAIAH 6:1-8

HOLY, HOLY, HOLY

Holy Father

Most Holy Place

Holy One of Israel

Holy One of Jacob

HOLY ONE
PSALM 16:7-11

Holiness

Holy One of God

Holy Servant Jesus

Holy Spirit

Spirit of Holiness

1 CORINTHIANS 6:9-20

PSALM 40:9-10

RIGHTEOUS GOD

Righteous Father

Righteous Judge

Righteous Servant

Holy and Righteous One

RIGHTEOUS ONE
2 CORINTHIANS 5:21

King of Righteousness

Lord Our Righteousness

Sun of Righteousness

Branch of Righteousness

Righteousness

ROMANS 1:16-17

PSALM 112

UPRIGHT ONE

Christ Jesus

Christ

Messiah

Pure

ANOINTED ONE
1 JOHN 1:7

Refiner and Purifier

Refiner's Fire

Oil

Soap of launderer

1 JOHN 3:1-3

1 THESSALONIANS 4:1-8

LEVITICUS 11:44-45

PSALM 51

CORRUPTION (GENESIS 6:5-6, 11-12)

insincerity   shadiness   cunning   hidden agenda   duplicity   sanctimony   lip service   two-faced   stab in back

misrepresentation   mismanage   misuse   dysfunctional   twisted   contorted   perversion   dishonorable   impure   contaminated

immodest   vulgar   obscene   pornography   prostitution   desecration   profanation   sacrilege

Set Apart by Design
Creative Responses to God, Jesus, Holy Spirit

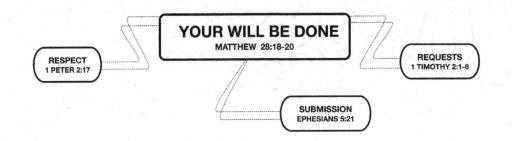

YOUR WILL BE DONE
MATTHEW 28:18-20

RESPECT
1 PETER 2:17

REQUESTS
1 TIMOTHY 2:1-8

SUBMISSION
EPHESIANS 5:21

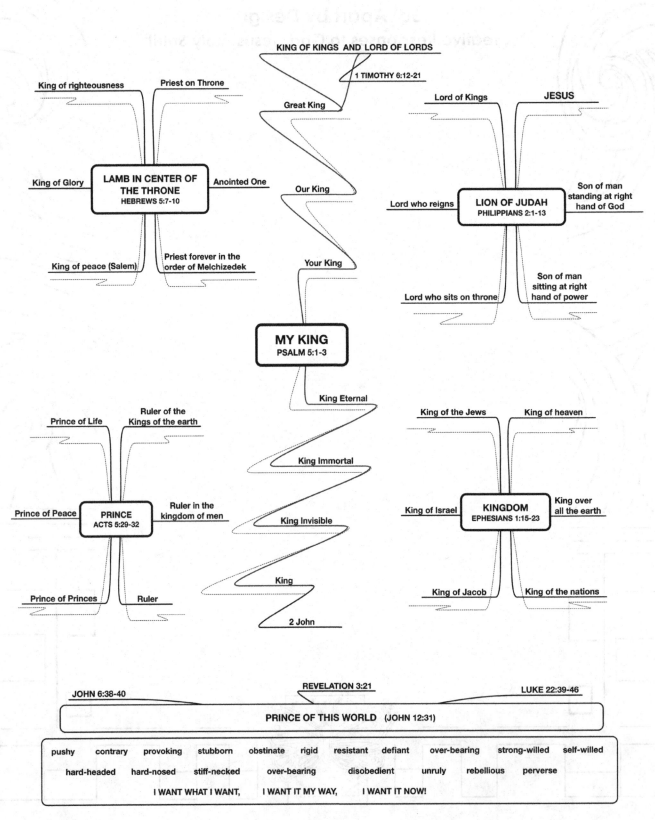

KING OF KINGS AND LORD OF LORDS

1 TIMOTHY 6:12-21

Great King

King of righteousness

Priest on Throne

Lord of Kings

JESUS

King of Glory

LAMB IN CENTER OF THE THRONE
HEBREWS 5:7-10

Anointed One

Our King

Lord who reigns

LION OF JUDAH
PHILIPPIANS 2:1-13

Son of man standing at right hand of God

King of peace (Salem)

Priest forever in the order of Melchizedek

Your King

Lord who sits on throne

Son of man sitting at right hand of power

MY KING
PSALM 5:1-3

King Eternal

Prince of Life

Ruler of the Kings of the earth

King of the Jews

King of heaven

King Immortal

Prince of Peace

PRINCE
ACTS 5:29-32

Ruler in the kingdom of men

King Invisible

King of Israel

KINGDOM
EPHESIANS 1:15-23

King over all the earth

Prince of Princes

Ruler

King

King of Jacob

King of the nations

2 John

JOHN 6:38-40

REVELATION 3:21

LUKE 22:39-46

PRINCE OF THIS WORLD (JOHN 12:31)

pushy   contrary   provoking   stubborn   obstinate   rigid   resistant   defiant   over-bearing   strong-willed   self-willed

hard-headed   hard-nosed   stiff-necked   over-bearing   disobedient   unruly   rebellious   perverse

I WANT WHAT I WANT,   I WANT IT MY WAY,   I WANT IT NOW!

Your Will Be Done
Creative Responses to God, Jesus, Holy Spirit

CHAPTER 2

Personal God: Humanity

List of Creative Clusters

Became Like Us

Child's Prayer

Father's Footsteps

Servant's Heart

Umbrella of Fellowship

Carrie's Joy: Shattered

(hurt)

Carrie's teacher told her students to bring a special object from home and share a story about it. Carrie excitedly found a small box and padded it with cotton for Joy's journey. Outside the school some bullies ripped the box out of Carrie's hands and crushed it under their feet. They threatened to beat Carrie if she told anyone. Something shattered inside Carrie. While her classmates shared their stories, she felt that there was something wrong with her. All she could think was, "Why did God allow the bullies to crush my Joy?"

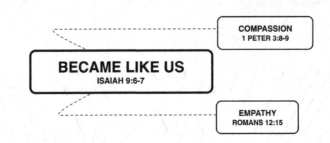

COMPASSION
1 PETER 3:8-9

BECAME LIKE US
ISAIAH 9:6-7

EMPATHY
ROMANS 12:15

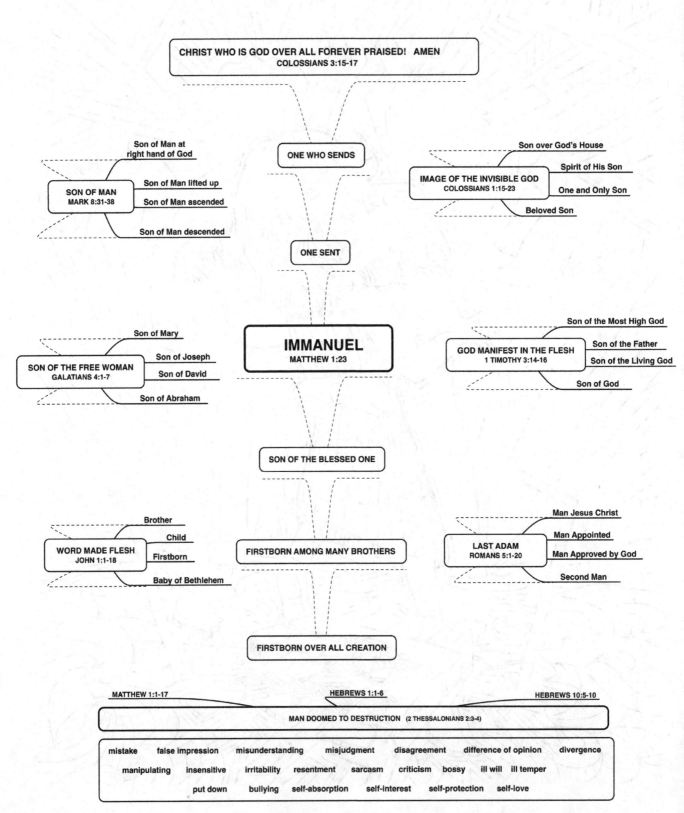

CHRIST WHO IS GOD OVER ALL FOREVER PRAISED! AMEN
COLOSSIANS 3:15-17

ONE WHO SENDS

Son of Man at right hand of God

SON OF MAN
MARK 8:31-38

Son of Man lifted up

Son of Man ascended

Son of Man descended

IMAGE OF THE INVISIBLE GOD
COLOSSIANS 1:15-23

Son over God's House

Spirit of His Son

One and Only Son

Beloved Son

ONE SENT

Son of Mary

SON OF THE FREE WOMAN
GALATIANS 4:1-7

Son of Joseph

Son of David

Son of Abraham

IMMANUEL
MATTHEW 1:23

GOD MANIFEST IN THE FLESH
1 TIMOTHY 3:14-16

Son of the Most High God

Son of the Father

Son of the Living God

Son of God

SON OF THE BLESSED ONE

Brother

WORD MADE FLESH
JOHN 1:1-18

Child

Firstborn

Baby of Bethlehem

FIRSTBORN AMONG MANY BROTHERS

LAST ADAM
ROMANS 5:1-20

Man Jesus Christ

Man Appointed

Man Approved by God

Second Man

FIRSTBORN OVER ALL CREATION

MATTHEW 1:1-17   HEBREWS 1:1-6   HEBREWS 10:5-10

MAN DOOMED TO DESTRUCTION (2 THESSALONIANS 2:3-4)

| mistake | false impression | misunderstanding | misjudgment | disagreement | difference of opinion | divergence |

manipulating   insensitive   irritability   resentment   sarcasm   criticism   bossy   ill will   ill temper

put down   bullying   self-absorption   self-interest   self-protection   self-love

Became Like Us
Creative Responses to God, Jesus, Holy Spirit

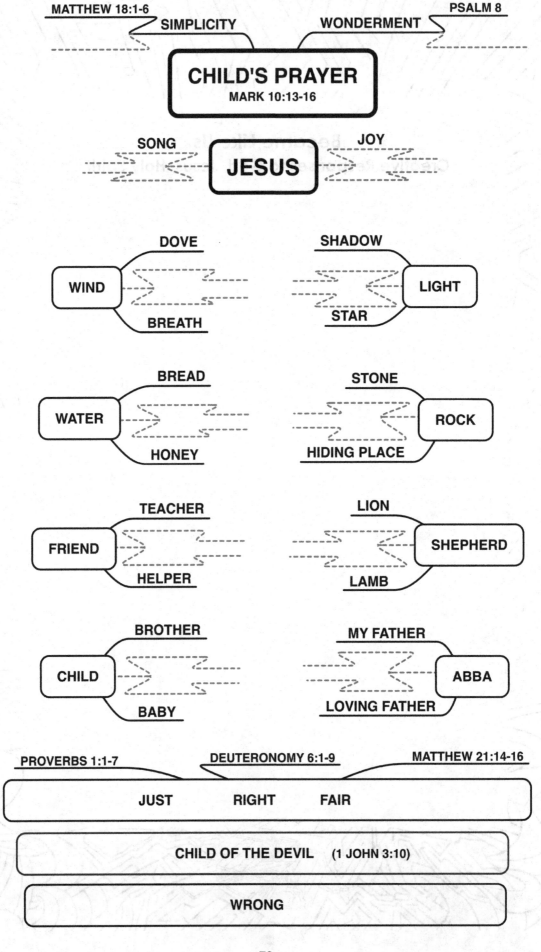

MATTHEW 18:1-6 SIMPLICITY WONDERMENT PSALM 8

CHILD'S PRAYER
MARK 10:13-16

SONG JOY

JESUS

DOVE
WIND
BREATH

SHADOW
LIGHT
STAR

BREAD
WATER
HONEY

STONE
ROCK
HIDING PLACE

TEACHER
FRIEND
HELPER

LION
SHEPHERD
LAMB

BROTHER
CHILD
BABY

MY FATHER
ABBA
LOVING FATHER

PROVERBS 1:1-7 DEUTERONOMY 6:1-9 MATTHEW 21:14-16

JUST RIGHT FAIR

CHILD OF THE DEVIL (1 JOHN 3:10)

WRONG

Child's Prayer
Creative Responses to God, Jesus, Holy Spirit

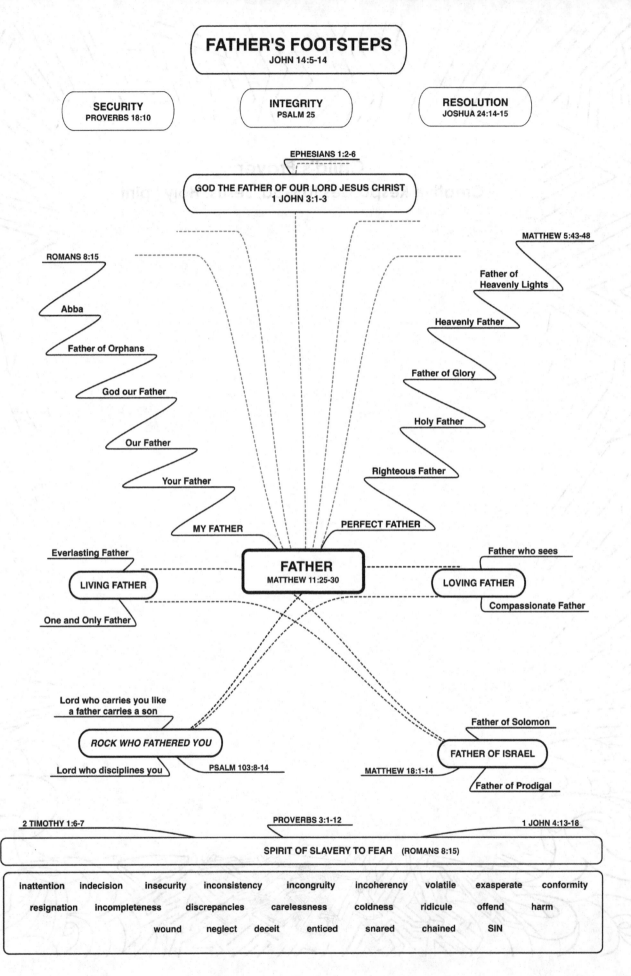

FATHER'S FOOTSTEPS
JOHN 14:5-14

SECURITY
PROVERBS 18:10

INTEGRITY
PSALM 25

RESOLUTION
JOSHUA 24:14-15

EPHESIANS 1:2-6

GOD THE FATHER OF OUR LORD JESUS CHRIST
1 JOHN 3:1-3

MATTHEW 5:43-48

ROMANS 8:15

Father of
Heavenly Lights

Abba

Heavenly Father

Father of Orphans

Father of Glory

God our Father

Holy Father

Our Father

Righteous Father

Your Father

MY FATHER   PERFECT FATHER

Everlasting Father   Father who sees

LIVING FATHER   **FATHER**   **LOVING FATHER**
                              MATTHEW 11:25-30

One and Only Father   Compassionate Father

Lord who carries you like
a father carries a son

Father of Solomon

ROCK WHO FATHERED YOU

FATHER OF ISRAEL

Lord who disciplines you   PSALM 103:8-14

MATTHEW 18:1-14

Father of Prodigal

2 TIMOTHY 1:6-7   PROVERBS 3:1-12   1 JOHN 4:13-18

SPIRIT OF SLAVERY TO FEAR   (ROMANS 8:15)

inattention   indecision   insecurity   inconsistency   incongruity   incoherency   volatile   exasperate   conformity

resignation   incompleteness   discrepancies   carelessness   coldness   ridicule   offend   harm

wound   neglect   deceit   enticed   snared   chained   SIN

Father's Footsteps
Creative Responses to God, Jesus, Holy Spirit

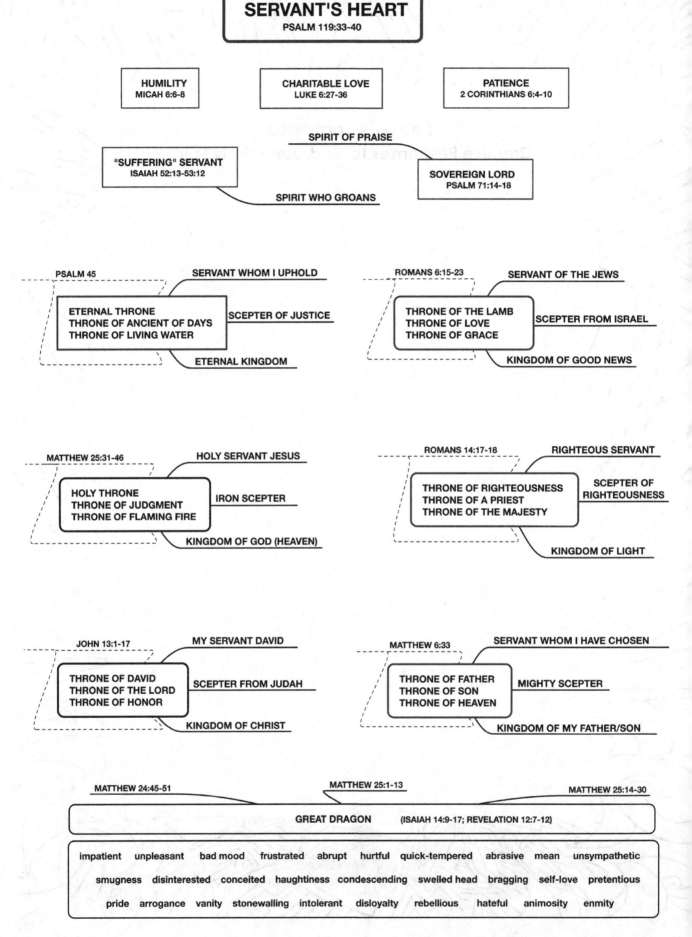

SERVANT'S HEART
PSALM 119:33-40

HUMILITY
MICAH 6:6-8

CHARITABLE LOVE
LUKE 6:27-36

PATIENCE
2 CORINTHIANS 6:4-10

SPIRIT OF PRAISE

"SUFFERING" SERVANT
ISAIAH 52:13-53:12

SOVEREIGN LORD
PSALM 71:14-18

SPIRIT WHO GROANS

PSALM 45 — SERVANT WHOM I UPHOLD

ETERNAL THRONE
THRONE OF ANCIENT OF DAYS
THRONE OF LIVING WATER

SCEPTER OF JUSTICE

ETERNAL KINGDOM

ROMANS 6:15-23 — SERVANT OF THE JEWS

THRONE OF THE LAMB
THRONE OF LOVE
THRONE OF GRACE

SCEPTER FROM ISRAEL

KINGDOM OF GOOD NEWS

MATTHEW 25:31-46 — HOLY SERVANT JESUS

HOLY THRONE
THRONE OF JUDGMENT
THRONE OF FLAMING FIRE

IRON SCEPTER

KINGDOM OF GOD (HEAVEN)

ROMANS 14:17-18 — RIGHTEOUS SERVANT

THRONE OF RIGHTEOUSNESS
THRONE OF A PRIEST
THRONE OF THE MAJESTY

SCEPTER OF RIGHTEOUSNESS

KINGDOM OF LIGHT

JOHN 13:1-17 — MY SERVANT DAVID

THRONE OF DAVID
THRONE OF THE LORD
THRONE OF HONOR

SCEPTER FROM JUDAH

KINGDOM OF CHRIST

MATTHEW 6:33 — SERVANT WHOM I HAVE CHOSEN

THRONE OF FATHER
THRONE OF SON
THRONE OF HEAVEN

MIGHTY SCEPTER

KINGDOM OF MY FATHER/SON

MATTHEW 24:45-51   MATTHEW 25:1-13   MATTHEW 25:14-30

GREAT DRAGON   (ISAIAH 14:9-17; REVELATION 12:7-12)

impatient   unpleasant   bad mood   frustrated   abrupt   hurtful   quick-tempered   abrasive   mean   unsympathetic

smugness   disinterested   conceited   haughtiness   condescending   swelled head   bragging   self-love   pretentious

pride   arrogance   vanity   stonewalling   intolerant   disloyalty   rebellious   hateful   animosity   enmity

76

Servant's Heart
Creative Responses to God, Jesus, Holy Spirit

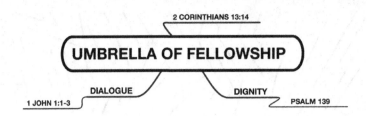

UMBRELLA OF FELLOWSHIP

2 CORINTHIANS 13:14

DIALOGUE   DIGNITY

1 JOHN 1:1-3   PSALM 139

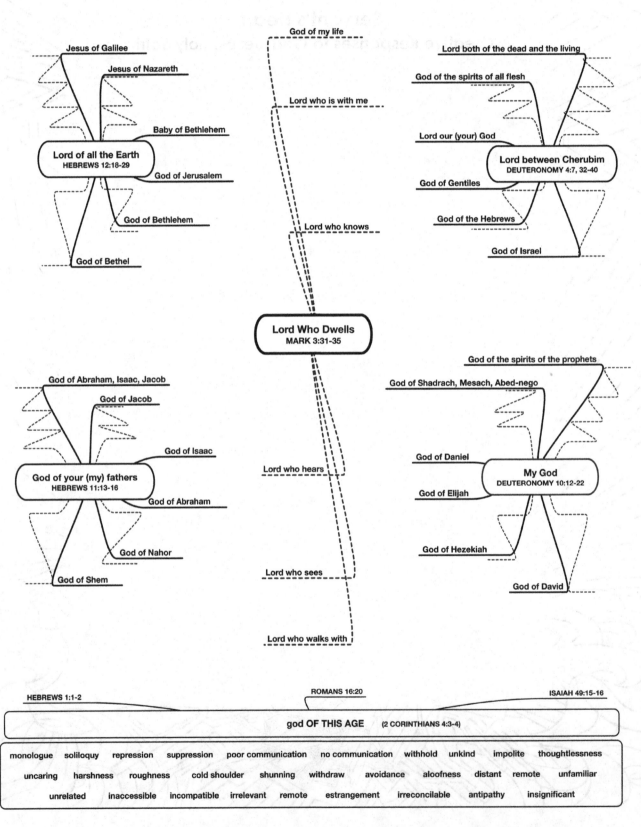

God of my life

Jesus of Galilee

Jesus of Nazareth

Baby of Bethlehem

Lord of all the Earth
HEBREWS 12:18-29

God of Jerusalem

God of Bethlehem

God of Bethel

Lord who is with me

Lord who knows

Lord both of the dead and the living

God of the spirits of all flesh

Lord our (your) God

Lord between Cherubim
DEUTERONOMY 4:7, 32-40

God of Gentiles

God of the Hebrews

God of Israel

Lord Who Dwells
MARK 3:31-35

God of Abraham, Isaac, Jacob

God of Jacob

God of Isaac

God of your (my) fathers
HEBREWS 11:13-16

God of Abraham

God of Nahor

God of Shem

Lord who hears

Lord who sees

Lord who walks with

God of the spirits of the prophets

God of Shadrach, Mesach, Abed-nego

God of Daniel

My God
DEUTERONOMY 10:12-22

God of Elijah

God of Hezekiah

God of David

HEBREWS 1:1-2   ROMANS 16:20   ISAIAH 49:15-16

god OF THIS AGE   (2 CORINTHIANS 4:3-4)

monologue   soliloquy   repression   suppression   poor communication   no communication   withhold   unkind   impolite   thoughtlessness

uncaring   harshness   roughness   cold shoulder   shunning   withdraw   avoidance   aloofness   distant   remote   unfamiliar

unrelated   inaccessible   incompatible   irrelevant   remote   estrangement   irreconcilable   antipathy   insignificant

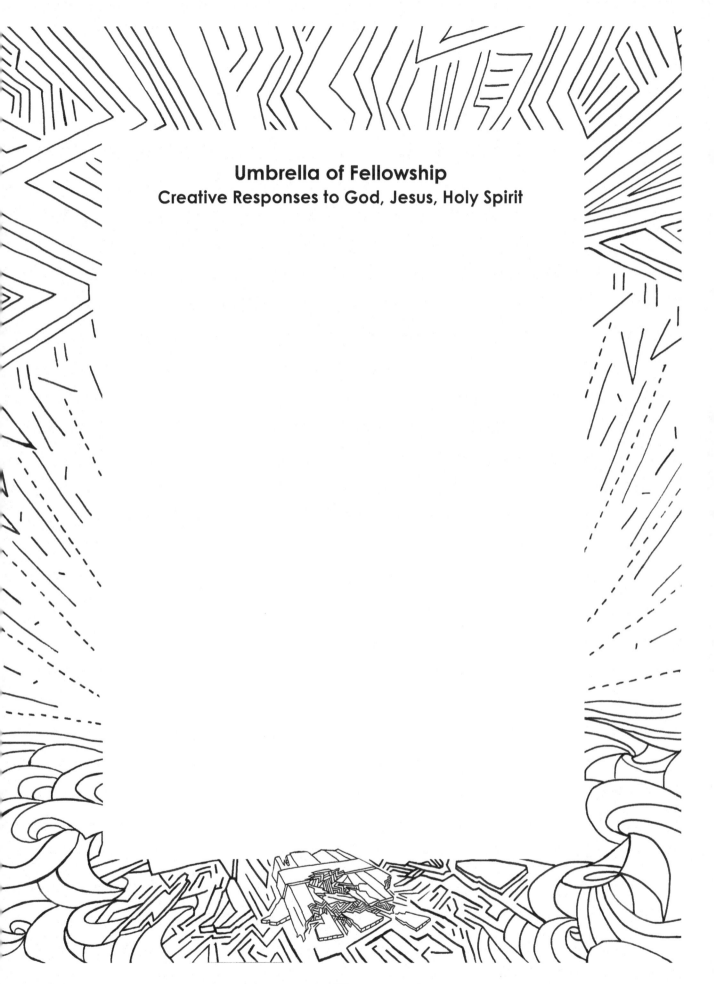

Umbrella of Fellowship
Creative Responses to God, Jesus, Holy Spirit

CHAPTER 3

God's Rescue: Salvation

List of Creative Clusters

Altar of Forgiveness

Gracious Promise

Marvelous in Our Eyes

Model of Suffering

Pathfinder

The Way of Truth

Carrie's Joy: Released

(gratitude)

Carrie sat by the butterfly haven day after day, crying. One day she saw two tear-shaped objects wiggling. Was someone crying with her? She named the shapes Hurt and Shame. All that year they grew bigger and bigger until one of them split open. A beautiful butterfly spread its wings and whispered, "My name is Freedom, not Hurt. You must forgive the bullies who crushed your Joy." It was the hardest thing Carrie ever had to do, but she did it. Freedom moved into her heart, but her unanswered question refused to move out. "Why did God allow the bullies to crush my Joy?"

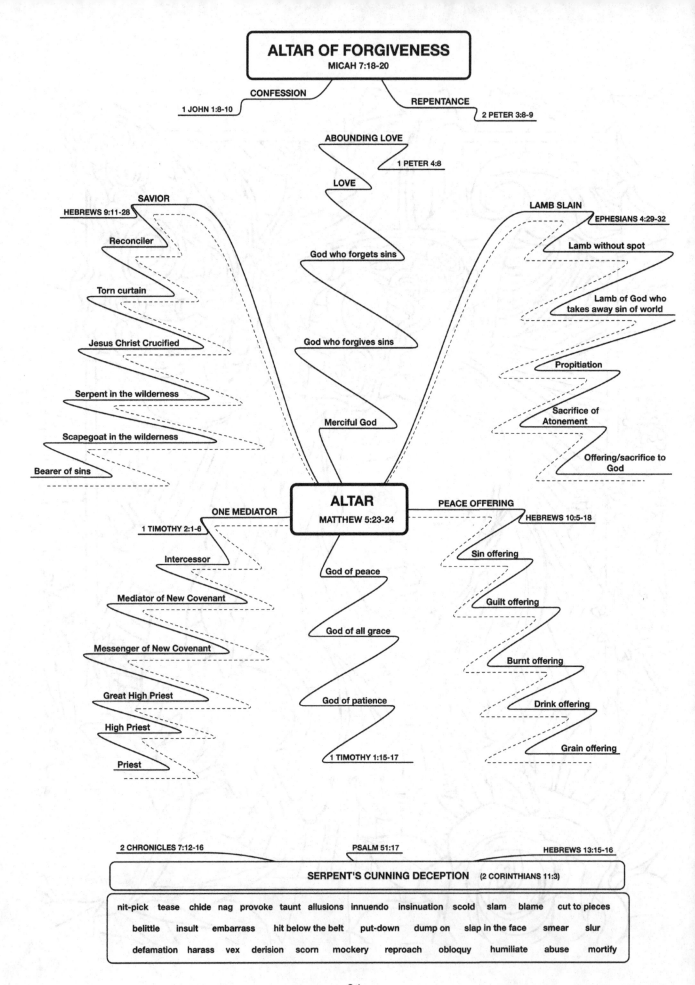

ALTAR OF FORGIVENESS
MICAH 7:18-20

CONFESSION
1 JOHN 1:8-10

REPENTANCE
2 PETER 3:8-9

ABOUNDING LOVE
1 PETER 4:8

LOVE

SAVIOR
HEBREWS 9:11-28

Reconciler

Torn curtain

Jesus Christ Crucified

Serpent in the wilderness

Scapegoat in the wilderness

Bearer of sins

God who forgets sins

God who forgives sins

Merciful God

LAMB SLAIN
EPHESIANS 4:29-32

Lamb without spot

Lamb of God who takes away sin of world

Propitiation

Sacrifice of Atonement

Offering/sacrifice to God

ALTAR
MATTHEW 5:23-24

ONE MEDIATOR
1 TIMOTHY 2:1-6

Intercessor

Mediator of New Covenant

Messenger of New Covenant

Great High Priest

High Priest

Priest

God of peace

God of all grace

God of patience

1 TIMOTHY 1:15-17

PEACE OFFERING
HEBREWS 10:5-18

Sin offering

Guilt offering

Burnt offering

Drink offering

Grain offering

2 CHRONICLES 7:12-16

PSALM 51:17

HEBREWS 13:15-16

SERPENT'S CUNNING DECEPTION   (2 CORINTHIANS 11:3)

nit-pick   tease   chide   nag   provoke   taunt   allusions   innuendo   insinuation   scold   slam   blame   cut to pieces

belittle   insult   embarrass   hit below the belt   put-down   dump on   slap in the face   smear   slur

defamation   harass   vex   derision   scorn   mockery   reproach   obloquy   humiliate   abuse   mortify

Altar of Forgiveness
Creative Responses to God, Jesus, Holy Spirit

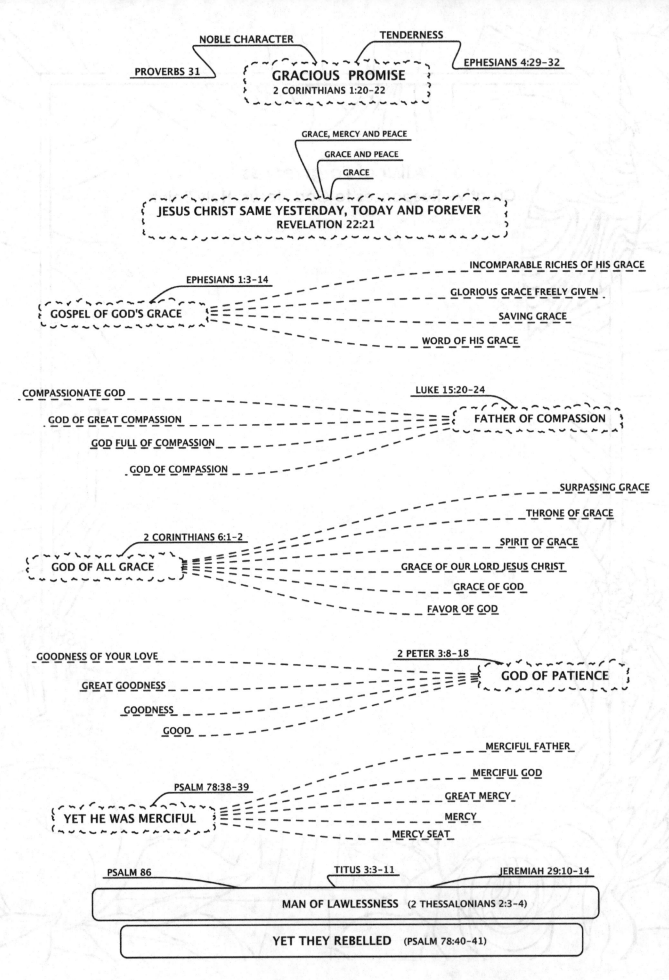

NOBLE CHARACTER   TENDERNESS

PROVERBS 31   **GRACIOUS PROMISE**   EPHESIANS 4:29–32
                     2 CORINTHIANS 1:20–22

GRACE, MERCY AND PEACE

GRACE AND PEACE

GRACE

JESUS CHRIST SAME YESTERDAY, TODAY AND FOREVER
REVELATION 22:21

EPHESIANS 1:3–14   INCOMPARABLE RICHES OF HIS GRACE

                                                   GLORIOUS GRACE FREELY GIVEN

GOSPEL OF GOD'S GRACE   SAVING GRACE

                                                   WORD OF HIS GRACE

COMPASSIONATE GOD   LUKE 15:20–24

GOD OF GREAT COMPASSION   **FATHER OF COMPASSION**

GOD FULL OF COMPASSION

GOD OF COMPASSION

                                                   SURPASSING GRACE

                                                   THRONE OF GRACE

2 CORINTHIANS 6:1–2   SPIRIT OF GRACE

GOD OF ALL GRACE   GRACE OF OUR LORD JESUS CHRIST

                                                   GRACE OF GOD

                                                   FAVOR OF GOD

GOODNESS OF YOUR LOVE   2 PETER 3:8–18

GREAT GOODNESS   **GOD OF PATIENCE**

GOODNESS

GOOD

                                                   MERCIFUL FATHER

                                                   MERCIFUL GOD

PSALM 78:38–39   GREAT MERCY

                                                   MERCY

YET HE WAS MERCIFUL   MERCY SEAT

PSALM 86   TITUS 3:3–11   JEREMIAH 29:10–14

MAN OF LAWLESSNESS (2 THESSALONIANS 2:3–4)

YET THEY REBELLED   (PSALM 78:40–41)

Gracious Promise
Creative Responses to God, Jesus, Holy Spirit

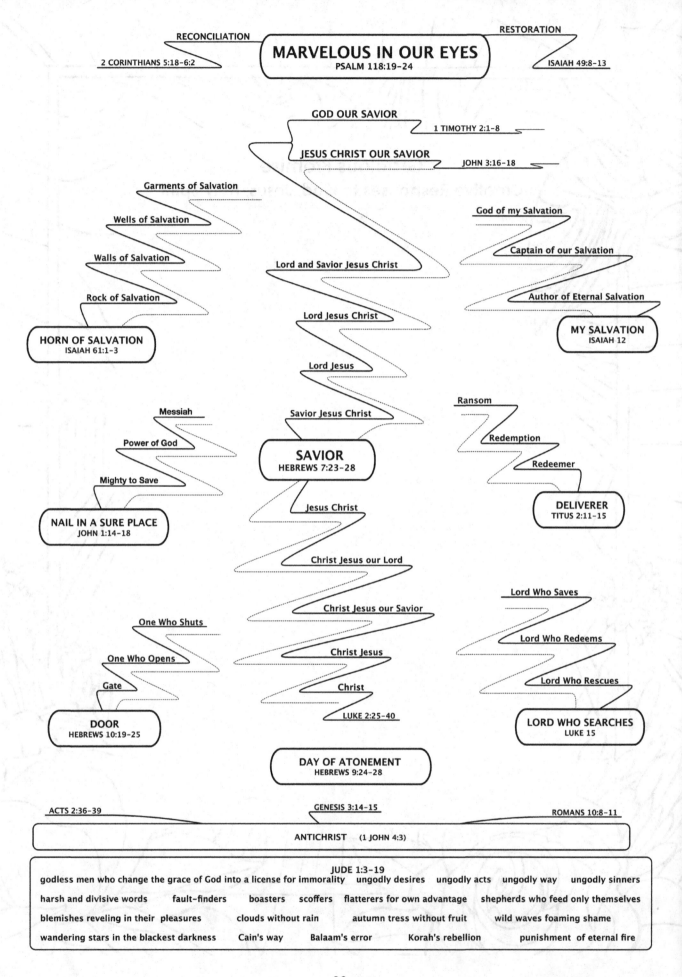

MARVELOUS IN OUR EYES
PSALM 118:19-24

RECONCILIATION

2 CORINTHIANS 5:18-6:2

RESTORATION

ISAIAH 49:8-13

GOD OUR SAVIOR

1 TIMOTHY 2:1-8

JESUS CHRIST OUR SAVIOR

JOHN 3:16-18

Garments of Salvation

Wells of Salvation

Walls of Salvation

Rock of Salvation

God of my Salvation

Captain of our Salvation

Author of Eternal Salvation

Lord and Savior Jesus Christ

Lord Jesus Christ

Lord Jesus

HORN OF SALVATION
ISAIAH 61:1-3

MY SALVATION
ISAIAH 12

Messiah

Power of God

Mighty to Save

Savior Jesus Christ

SAVIOR
HEBREWS 7:23-28

Jesus Christ

Ransom

Redemption

Redeemer

NAIL IN A SURE PLACE
JOHN 1:14-18

DELIVERER
TITUS 2:11-15

Christ Jesus our Lord

Christ Jesus our Savior

One Who Shuts

One Who Opens

Gate

Christ Jesus

Christ

Lord Who Saves

Lord Who Redeems

Lord Who Rescues

DOOR
HEBREWS 10:19-25

LUKE 2:25-40

LORD WHO SEARCHES
LUKE 15

DAY OF ATONEMENT
HEBREWS 9:24-28

ACTS 2:36-39

GENESIS 3:14-15

ROMANS 10:8-11

ANTICHRIST (1 JOHN 4:3)

JUDE 1:3-19
godless men who change the grace of God into a license for immorality   ungodly desires   ungodly acts   ungodly way   ungodly sinners

harsh and divisive words   fault-finders   boasters   scoffers   flatterers for own advantage   shepherds who feed only themselves

blemishes reveling in their pleasures   clouds without rain   autumn tress without fruit   wild waves foaming shame

wandering stars in the blackest darkness   Cain's way   Balaam's error   Korah's rebellion   punishment of eternal fire

Marvelous in Our Eyes
Creative Responses to God, Jesus, Holy Spirit

MODEL OF SUFFERING
HEBREWS 12:1-4

SIGNIFICANCE	JOY	MEDITATION
JOB 42:1-6	2 CORINTHIANS 12:9-10	PSALM 119:9-32

One slapped in the face · One blindfolded · One beaten with fists · One pierced

HEBREWS 11:25-26 · One spat upon · One flogged · PHILIPPIANS 1:27-30

MAN OF SORROWS
HEBREWS 4:14-16

One disowned · One abandoned · One accused · One mocked

1 PETER 5:8-11 · One betrayed · One anguished · One despised · One insulted · MATTHEW 5:11-12

FEAR OF ISAAC JOHN 15:12-17	Bearer of Sins	Sin Offering	Reproach of Men

STRANGER HEBREWS 13:1-2	Alien	Guest	Nazarene

TORN CURTAIN REVELATION 5:8-14	Crown of Thorns	Blood Poured Out	Body Given

WORM 1 PETER 2:11-12	Owl of the Desert	Bronze Serpent in the Wilderness	Scapegoat in the wilderness

STONE OF STUMBLING PSALM 55	Rejected Stone	Rock of Offense	Trap (Snare)

ROMANS 16:17-19 · JAMES 4:1-10 · 1 JOHN 2:15-17

ANGEL OF LIGHT (2 CORINTHIANS 11:14-15)

Epicureanism	Sybaritism	Hedonism	Humanism	Relativism
worldly pleasures	intemperance · coveting	indulgence	over-indulgence · gluttony	lewdness · lust

"If it feels good, do it"   "If it works, do it"   "It's my life, I'll decide"

"Why not?   "WHO ARE YOU TO TELL ME?"

Model of Suffering
Creative Responses to God, Jesus, Holy Spirit

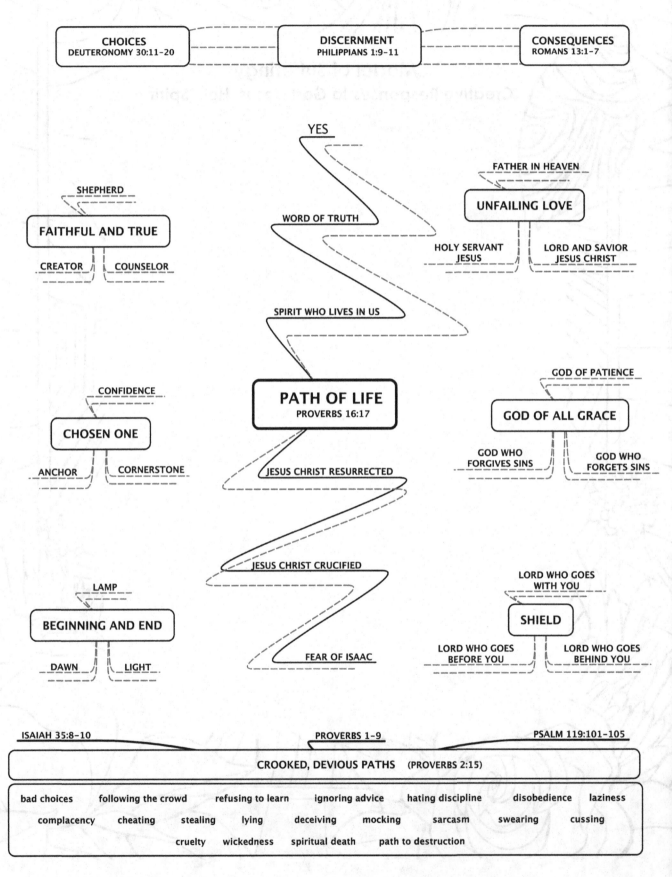

PATHFINDER
JOHN 14:4-6

CHOICES
DEUTERONOMY 30:11-20

DISCERNMENT
PHILIPPIANS 1:9-11

CONSEQUENCES
ROMANS 13:1-7

YES

SHEPHERD

WORD OF TRUTH

FATHER IN HEAVEN

FAITHFUL AND TRUE

UNFAILING LOVE

CREATOR   COUNSELOR

HOLY SERVANT
JESUS

LORD AND SAVIOR
JESUS CHRIST

SPIRIT WHO LIVES IN US

CONFIDENCE

GOD OF PATIENCE

CHOSEN ONE

PATH OF LIFE
PROVERBS 16:17

GOD OF ALL GRACE

ANCHOR   CORNERSTONE

GOD WHO
FORGIVES SINS

GOD WHO
FORGETS SINS

JESUS CHRIST RESURRECTED

LORD WHO GOES
WITH YOU

LAMP

JESUS CHRIST CRUCIFIED

SHIELD

BEGINNING AND END

DAWN   LIGHT

FEAR OF ISAAC

LORD WHO GOES
BEFORE YOU

LORD WHO GOES
BEHIND YOU

ISAIAH 35:8-10

PROVERBS 1-9

PSALM 119:101-105

CROOKED, DEVIOUS PATHS   (PROVERBS 2:15)

bad choices   following the crowd   refusing to learn   ignoring advice   hating discipline   disobedience   laziness

complacency   cheating   stealing   lying   deceiving   mocking   sarcasm   swearing   cussing

cruelty   wickedness   spiritual death   path to destruction

Pathfinder
Creative Responses to God, Jesus, Holy Spirit

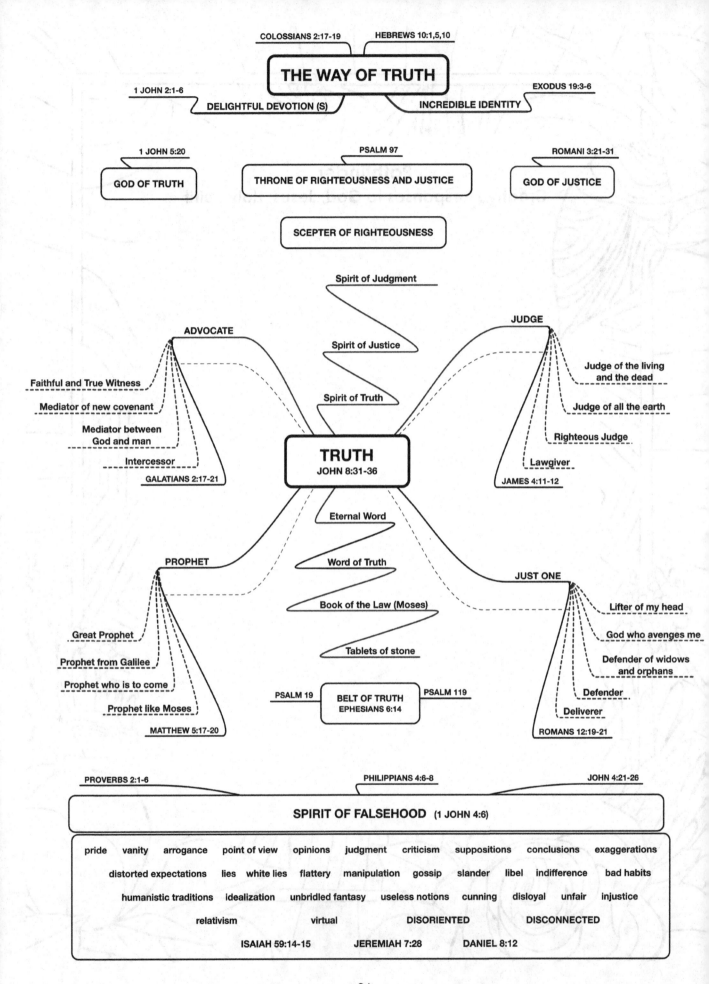

THE WAY OF TRUTH

COLOSSIANS 2:17-19   HEBREWS 10:1,5,10

1 JOHN 2:1-6
DELIGHTFUL DEVOTION (S)   INCREDIBLE IDENTITY   EXODUS 19:3-6

1 JOHN 5:20
GOD OF TRUTH

PSALM 97
THRONE OF RIGHTEOUSNESS AND JUSTICE

ROMANI 3:21-31
GOD OF JUSTICE

SCEPTER OF RIGHTEOUSNESS

Spirit of Judgment

ADVOCATE   JUDGE

Spirit of Justice

Faithful and True Witness   Judge of the living
                                                    and the dead
Mediator of new covenant
                                                    Judge of all the earth
Spirit of Truth
Mediator between
God and man   Righteous Judge

Intercessor   Lawgiver

GALATIANS 2:17-21   JAMES 4:11-12

TRUTH
JOHN 8:31-36

Eternal Word

PROPHET   Word of Truth   JUST ONE

                            Book of the Law (Moses)   Lifter of my head

Great Prophet   God who avenges me

Prophet from Galilee   Tablets of stone   Defender of widows
                                                    and orphans
Prophet who is to come
                                                    Defender
                   PSALM 19   BELT OF TRUTH   PSALM 119
Prophet like Moses   EPHESIANS 6:14   Deliverer

MATTHEW 5:17-20   ROMANS 12:19-21

PROVERBS 2:1-6   PHILIPPIANS 4:6-8   JOHN 4:21-26

SPIRIT OF FALSEHOOD (1 JOHN 4:6)

pride   vanity   arrogance   point of view   opinions   judgment   criticism   suppositions   conclusions   exaggerations

distorted expectations   lies   white lies   flattery   manipulation   gossip   slander   libel   indifference   bad habits

humanistic traditions   idealization   unbridled fantasy   useless notions   cunning   disloyal   unfair   injustice

relativism   virtual   DISORIENTED   DISCONNECTED

ISAIAH 59:14-15   JEREMIAH 7:28   DANIEL 8:12

96

The Way of Truth
Creative Responses to God, Jesus, Holy Spirit

CHAPTER 4

God's Power: Living Inside Out

List of Creative Clusters

Called to Be

Christlikeness

Effective Ministry

Spiritual Warfare

Valley of Decision

Carrie's Joy: Strengthened

(impatience)

Carrie grew very impatient while waiting for Shame to transform itself. Maybe the answer to her question was tucked into the second cocoon. She grabbed her scissors to help it out, but Freedom stopped her.

"What is living inside can't be forced from the outside. Be patient." It seemed like forever before the second cocoon suddenly burst open.

An even larger butterfly flew toward Carrie and confided, "My name is Grace, not Shame. If you want to find the answer to your question about why God allowed the bullies to crush Joy, we can travel together to the Father's heart."

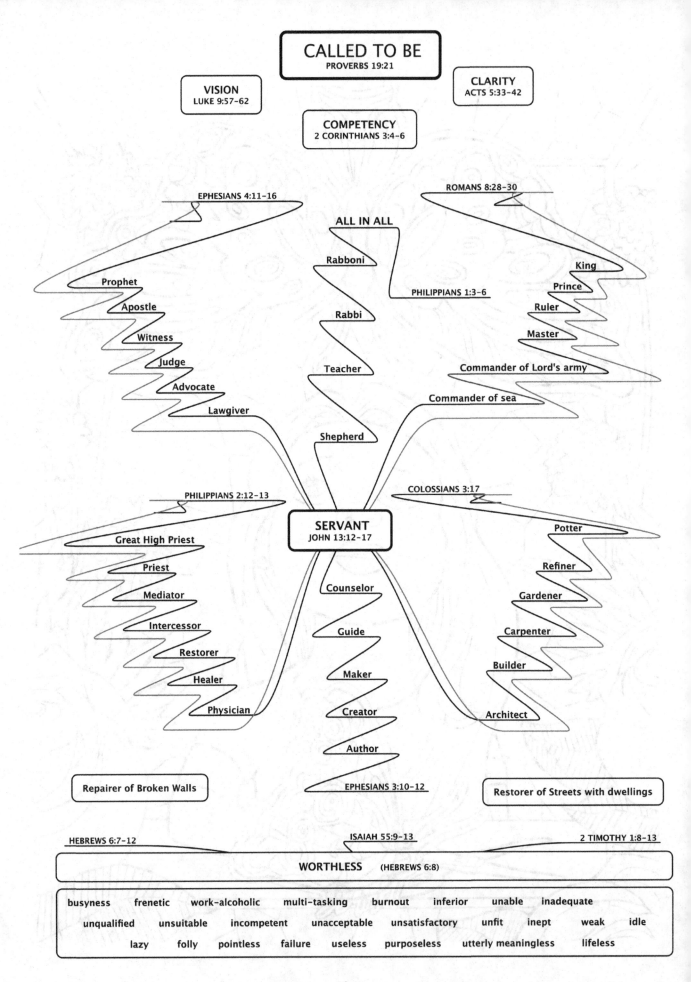

CALLED TO BE
PROVERBS 19:21

VISION
LUKE 9:57–62

CLARITY
ACTS 5:33–42

COMPETENCY
2 CORINTHIANS 3:4–6

EPHESIANS 4:11–16

ROMANS 8:28–30

ALL IN ALL

Rabboni

King

Prince

PHILIPPIANS 1:3–6

Ruler

Rabbi

Master

Prophet

Apostle

Witness

Judge

Commander of Lord's army

Advocate

Teacher

Commander of sea

Lawgiver

Shepherd

PHILIPPIANS 2:12–13

COLOSSIANS 3:17

SERVANT
JOHN 13:12–17

Potter

Great High Priest

Refiner

Priest

Gardener

Mediator

Counselor

Intercessor

Guide

Carpenter

Restorer

Builder

Healer

Maker

Physician

Creator

Architect

Author

Repairer of Broken Walls

EPHESIANS 3:10–12

Restorer of Streets with dwellings

HEBREWS 6:7–12

ISAIAH 55:9–13

2 TIMOTHY 1:8–13

WORTHLESS (HEBREWS 6:8)

busyness   frenetic   work-alcoholic   multi-tasking   burnout   inferior   unable   inadequate

unqualified   unsuitable   incompetent   unacceptable   unsatisfactory   unfit   inept   weak   idle

lazy   folly   pointless   failure   useless   purposeless   utterly meaningless   lifeless

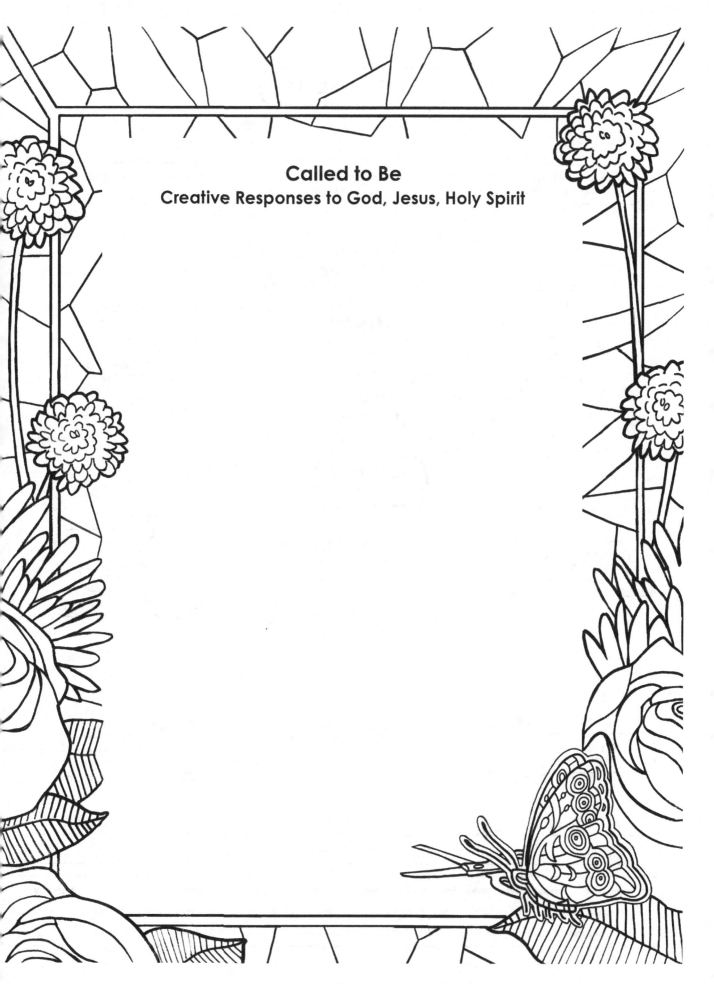

Called to Be
Creative Responses to God, Jesus, Holy Spirit

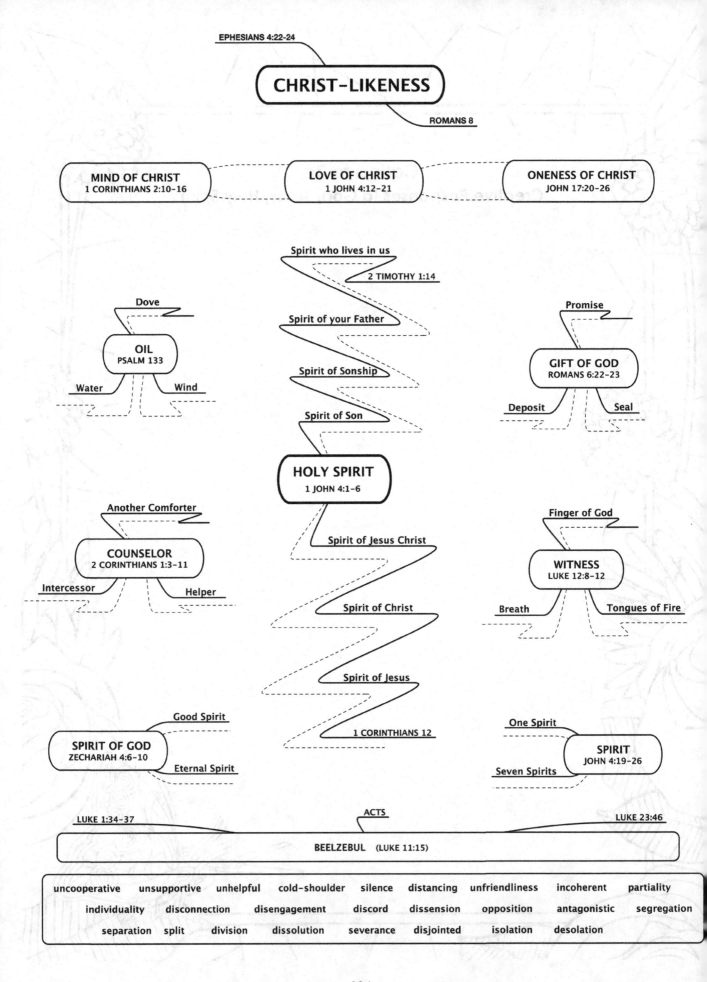

EPHESIANS 4:22-24

CHRIST-LIKENESS

ROMANS 8

MIND OF CHRIST
1 CORINTHIANS 2:10-16

LOVE OF CHRIST
1 JOHN 4:12-21

ONENESS OF CHRIST
JOHN 17:20-26

Spirit who lives in us

2 TIMOTHY 1:14

Spirit of your Father

Spirit of Sonship

Spirit of Son

Dove

OIL
PSALM 133

Water   Wind

Promise

GIFT OF GOD
ROMANS 6:22-23

Deposit   Seal

HOLY SPIRIT
1 JOHN 4:1-6

Another Comforter

COUNSELOR
2 CORINTHIANS 1:3-11

Intercessor   Helper

Spirit of Jesus Christ

Spirit of Christ

Spirit of Jesus

1 CORINTHIANS 12

Finger of God

WITNESS
LUKE 12:8-12

Breath   Tongues of Fire

Good Spirit

SPIRIT OF GOD
ZECHARIAH 4:6-10

Eternal Spirit

One Spirit

SPIRIT
JOHN 4:19-26

Seven Spirits

LUKE 1:34-37   ACTS   LUKE 23:46

BEELZEBUL (LUKE 11:15)

uncooperative   unsupportive   unhelpful   cold-shoulder   silence   distancing   unfriendliness   incoherent   partiality

individuality   disconnection   disengagement   discord   dissension   opposition   antagonistic   segregation

separation   split   division   dissolution   severance   disjointed   isolation   desolation

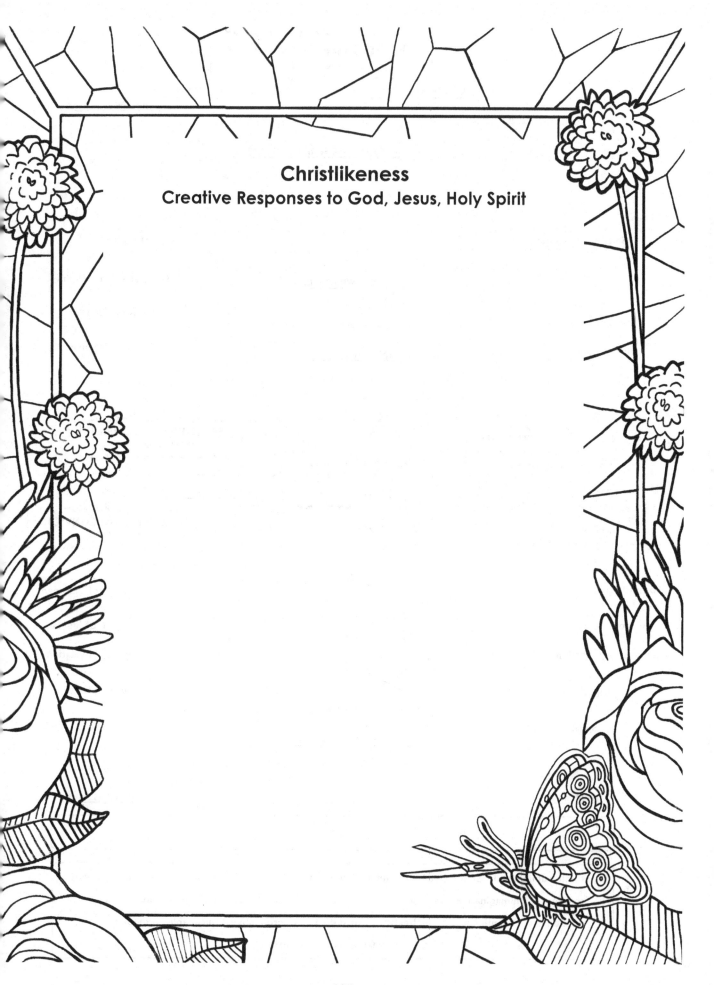

Christlikeness
Creative Responses to God, Jesus, Holy Spirit

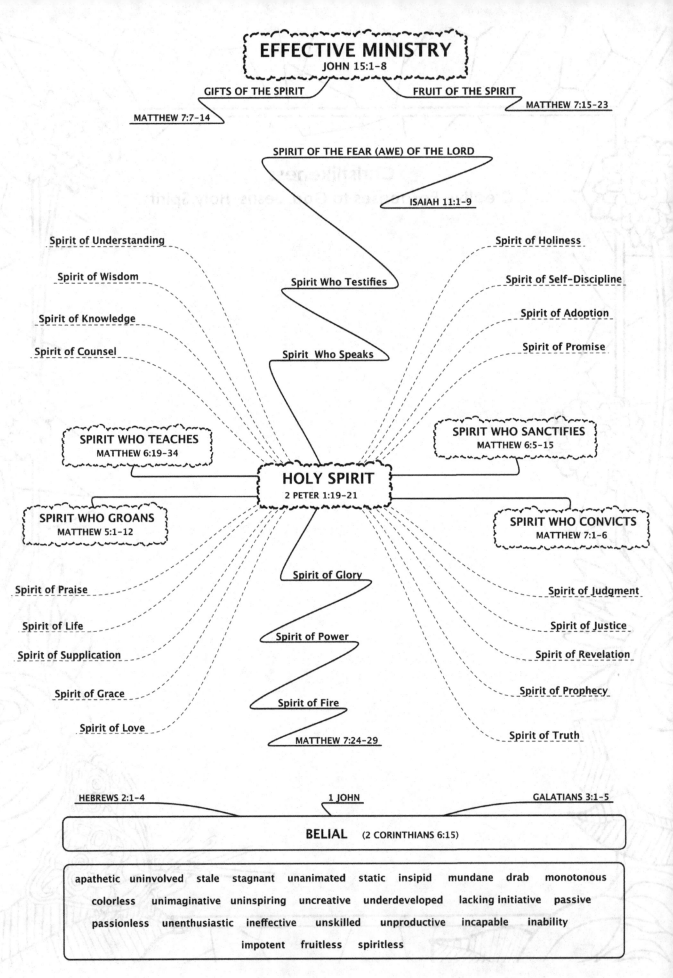

EFFECTIVE MINISTRY
JOHN 15:1-8

GIFTS OF THE SPIRIT   FRUIT OF THE SPIRIT

MATTHEW 7:7-14   MATTHEW 7:15-23

SPIRIT OF THE FEAR (AWE) OF THE LORD

ISAIAH 11:1-9

Spirit of Understanding

Spirit of Wisdom

Spirit of Knowledge

Spirit of Counsel

Spirit Who Testifies

Spirit Who Speaks

Spirit of Holiness

Spirit of Self-Discipline

Spirit of Adoption

Spirit of Promise

SPIRIT WHO TEACHES
MATTHEW 6:19-34

SPIRIT WHO SANCTIFIES
MATTHEW 6:5-15

HOLY SPIRIT
2 PETER 1:19-21

SPIRIT WHO GROANS
MATTHEW 5:1-12

SPIRIT WHO CONVICTS
MATTHEW 7:1-6

Spirit of Praise

Spirit of Life

Spirit of Supplication

Spirit of Grace

Spirit of Love

Spirit of Glory

Spirit of Power

Spirit of Fire

MATTHEW 7:24-29

Spirit of Judgment

Spirit of Justice

Spirit of Revelation

Spirit of Prophecy

Spirit of Truth

HEBREWS 2:1-4   1 JOHN   GALATIANS 3:1-5

BELIAL   (2 CORINTHIANS 6:15)

apathetic   uninvolved   stale   stagnant   unanimated   static   insipid   mundane   drab   monotonous

colorless   unimaginative   uninspiring   uncreative   underdeveloped   lacking initiative   passive

passionless   unenthusiastic   ineffective   unskilled   unproductive   incapable   inability

impotent   fruitless   spiritless

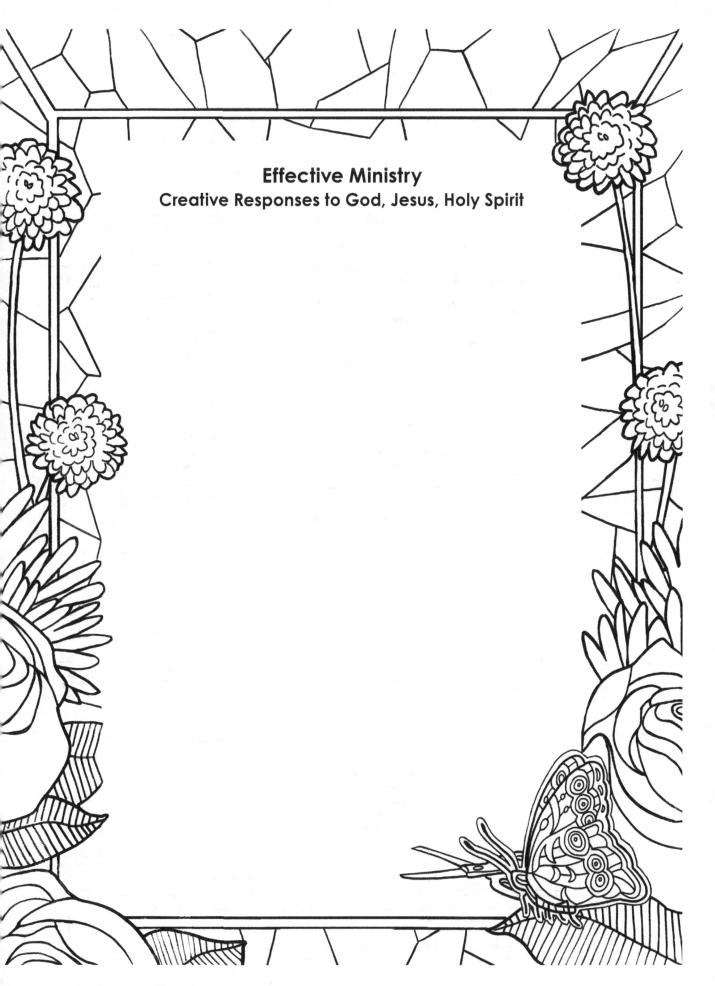

Effective Ministry
Creative Responses to God, Jesus, Holy Spirit

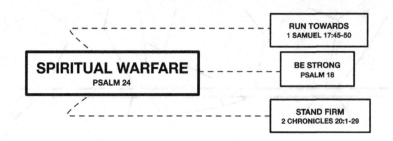

SPIRITUAL WARFARE
PSALM 24

RUN TOWARDS
1 SAMUEL 17:45-50

BE STRONG
PSALM 18

STAND FIRM
2 CHRONICLES 20:1-29

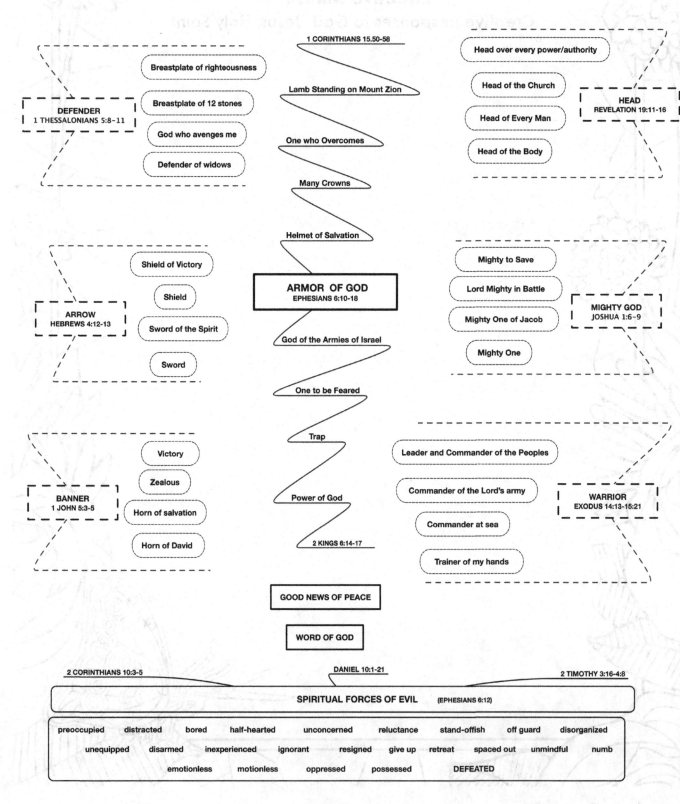

1 CORINTHIANS 15.50-58

Lamb Standing on Mount Zion

One who Overcomes

Many Crowns

Helmet of Salvation

ARMOR OF GOD
EPHESIANS 6:10-18

God of the Armies of Israel

One to be Feared

Trap

Power of God

2 KINGS 6:14-17

DEFENDER
1 THESSALONIANS 5:8-11

Breastplate of righteousness

Breastplate of 12 stones

God who avenges me

Defender of widows

HEAD
REVELATION 19:11-16

Head over every power/authority

Head of the Church

Head of Every Man

Head of the Body

ARROW
HEBREWS 4:12-13

Shield of Victory

Shield

Sword of the Spirit

Sword

MIGHTY GOD
JOSHUA 1:6-9

Mighty to Save

Lord Mighty in Battle

Mighty One of Jacob

Mighty One

BANNER
1 JOHN 5:3-5

Victory

Zealous

Horn of salvation

Horn of David

WARRIOR
EXODUS 14:13-15:21

Leader and Commander of the Peoples

Commander of the Lord's army

Commander at sea

Trainer of my hands

GOOD NEWS OF PEACE

WORD OF GOD

2 CORINTHIANS 10:3-5   DANIEL 10:1-21   2 TIMOTHY 3:16-4:8

SPIRITUAL FORCES OF EVIL   (EPHESIANS 6:12)

preoccupied   distracted   bored   half-hearted   unconcerned   reluctance   stand-offish   off guard   disorganized

unequipped   disarmed   inexperienced   ignorant   resigned   give up   retreat   spaced out   unmindful   numb

emotionless   motionless   oppressed   possessed   **DEFEATED**

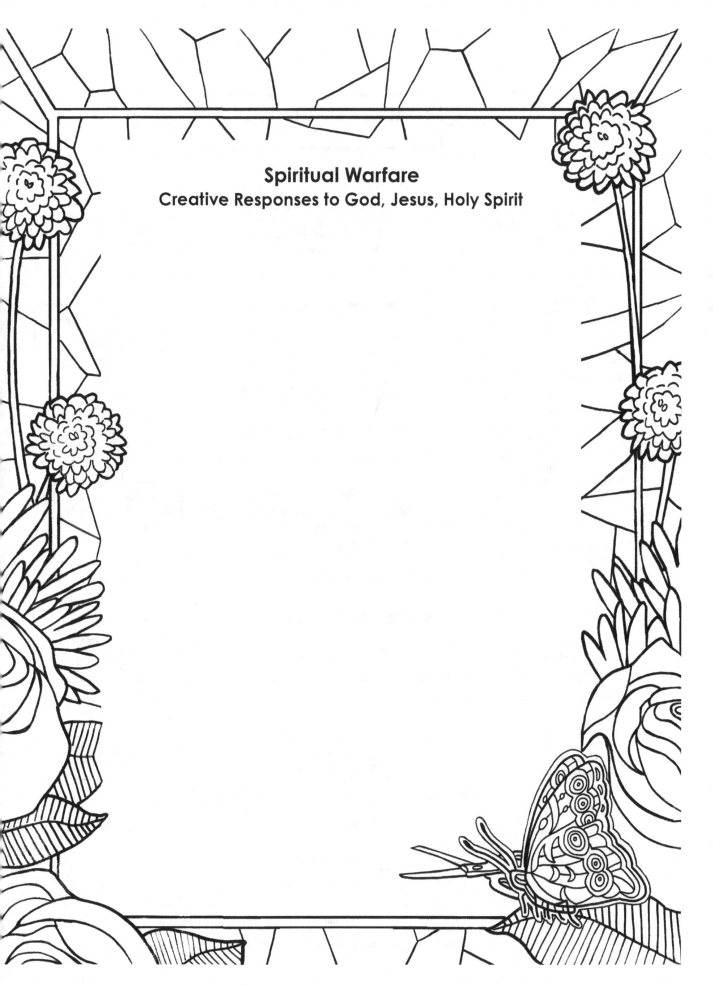

Spiritual Warfare
Creative Responses to God, Jesus, Holy Spirit

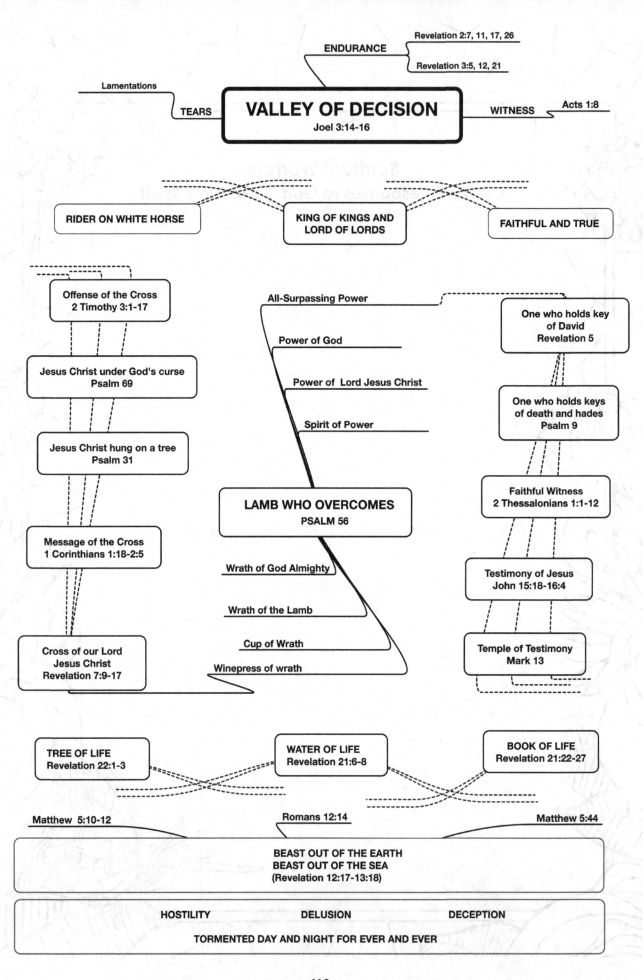

ENDURANCE
Revelation 2:7, 11, 17, 26
Revelation 3:5, 12, 21

Lamentations

TEARS

VALLEY OF DECISION
Joel 3:14-16

WITNESS   Acts 1:8

RIDER ON WHITE HORSE

KING OF KINGS AND
LORD OF LORDS

FAITHFUL AND TRUE

Offense of the Cross
2 Timothy 3:1-17

All-Surpassing Power

One who holds key
of David
Revelation 5

Power of God

Jesus Christ under God's curse
Psalm 69

Power of Lord Jesus Christ

One who holds keys
of death and hades
Psalm 9

Spirit of Power

Jesus Christ hung on a tree
Psalm 31

Faithful Witness
2 Thessalonians 1:1-12

LAMB WHO OVERCOMES
PSALM 56

Message of the Cross
1 Corinthians 1:18-2:5

Wrath of God Almighty

Testimony of Jesus
John 15:18-16:4

Wrath of the Lamb

Cross of our Lord
Jesus Christ
Revelation 7:9-17

Cup of Wrath

Temple of Testimony
Mark 13

Winepress of wrath

TREE OF LIFE
Revelation 22:1-3

WATER OF LIFE
Revelation 21:6-8

BOOK OF LIFE
Revelation 21:22-27

Matthew 5:10-12

Romans 12:14

Matthew 5:44

BEAST OUT OF THE EARTH
BEAST OUT OF THE SEA
(Revelation 12:17-13:18)

HOSTILITY   DELUSION   DECEPTION

TORMENTED DAY AND NIGHT FOR EVER AND EVER

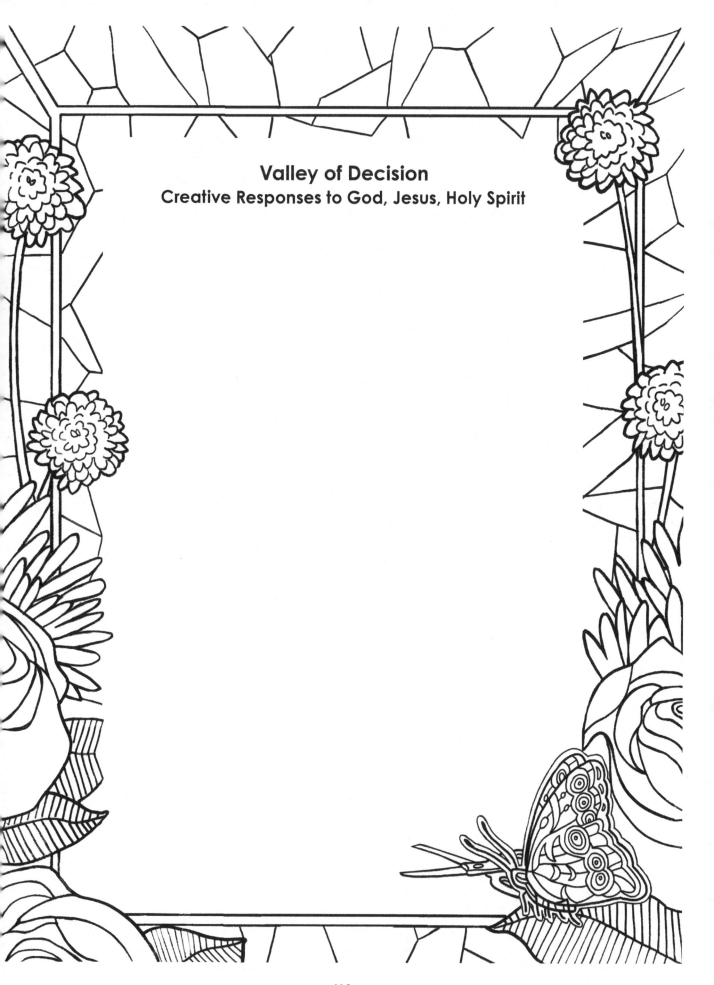

Valley of Decision
Creative Responses to God, Jesus, Holy Spirit

CHAPTER 5

God's Rest: Priorities

List of Creative Clusters

Anchored in Hope

Face-to-Face

Peacemaker

Rock-Solid Faith

Rooted in Love

Carrie's Joy: Challenged

(perseverance)

Carrie, Freedom, and Grace started on their journey to climb the highest mountain ever. Immediately they were surrounded by darkness and all kinds of obstacles. Whenever they got lost (which happened often), they would look up to the stars that pointed the way. Even though she was tired from pushing back against all her doubts and fears, Carrie cared for her friends' needs. Her last steps up the mountain proved to be the hardest. How she wished she could fly like Freedom and Grace. Maybe she could have flown if it weren't for the weight of her question, "Why did God allow the bullies to crush my Joy?"

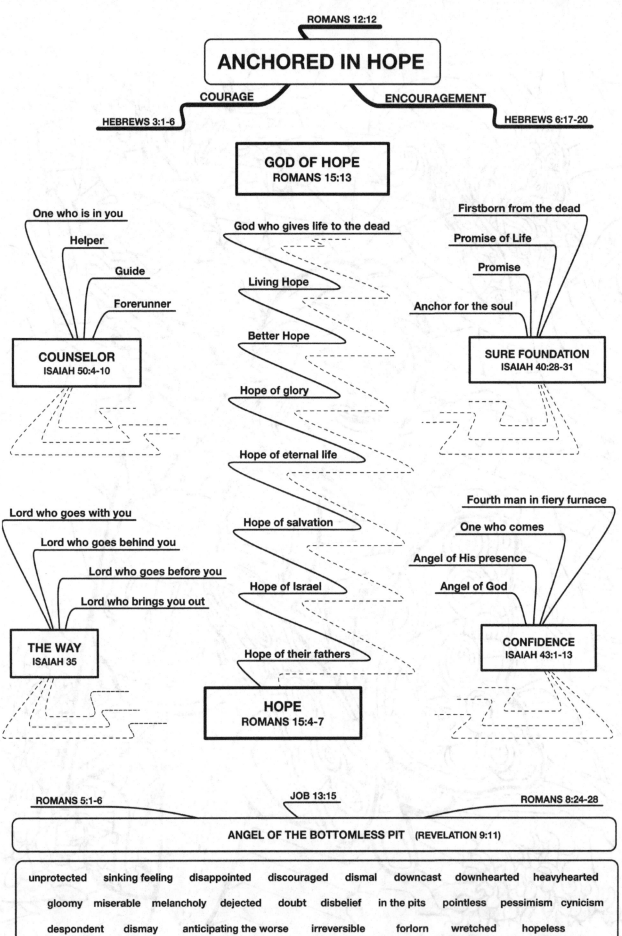

ROMANS 12:12

ANCHORED IN HOPE

COURAGE   ENCOURAGEMENT

HEBREWS 3:1-6   HEBREWS 6:17-20

GOD OF HOPE
ROMANS 15:13

One who is in you

God who gives life to the dead

Firstborn from the dead

Helper

Promise of Life

Guide

Living Hope

Promise

Forerunner

Better Hope

Anchor for the soul

COUNSELOR
ISAIAH 50:4-10

Hope of glory

SURE FOUNDATION
ISAIAH 40:28-31

Hope of eternal life

Fourth man in fiery furnace

Lord who goes with you

Hope of salvation

One who comes

Lord who goes behind you

Angel of His presence

Lord who goes before you

Hope of Israel

Angel of God

Lord who brings you out

THE WAY
ISAIAH 35

Hope of their fathers

CONFIDENCE
ISAIAH 43:1-13

HOPE
ROMANS 15:4-7

ROMANS 5:1-6   JOB 13:15   ROMANS 8:24-28

ANGEL OF THE BOTTOMLESS PIT   (REVELATION 9:11)

unprotected   sinking feeling   disappointed   discouraged   dismal   downcast   downhearted   heavyhearted

gloomy   miserable   melancholy   dejected   doubt   disbelief   in the pits   pointless   pessimism   cynicism

despondent   dismay   anticipating the worse   irreversible   forlorn   wretched   hopeless

120

Anchored in Hope
Creative Responses to God, Jesus, Holy Spirit

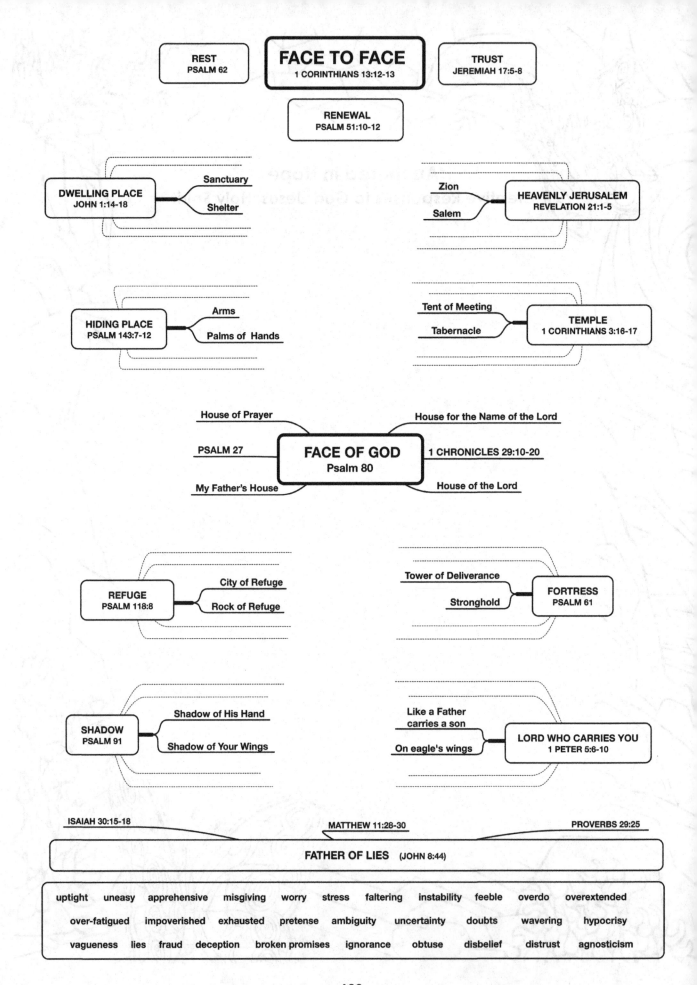

FACE TO FACE
1 CORINTHIANS 13:12-13

REST
PSALM 62

TRUST
JEREMIAH 17:5-8

RENEWAL
PSALM 51:10-12

DWELLING PLACE
JOHN 1:14-18
Sanctuary
Shelter

Zion
Salem
HEAVENLY JERUSALEM
REVELATION 21:1-5

HIDING PLACE
PSALM 143:7-12
Arms
Palms of Hands

Tent of Meeting
Tabernacle
TEMPLE
1 CORINTHIANS 3:16-17

House of Prayer
PSALM 27
FACE OF GOD
Psalm 80
House for the Name of the Lord
1 CHRONICLES 29:10-20
My Father's House
House of the Lord

REFUGE
PSALM 118:8
City of Refuge
Rock of Refuge

Tower of Deliverance
Stronghold
FORTRESS
PSALM 61

SHADOW
PSALM 91
Shadow of His Hand
Shadow of Your Wings

Like a Father
carries a son
On eagle's wings
LORD WHO CARRIES YOU
1 PETER 5:6-10

ISAIAH 30:15-18   MATTHEW 11:28-30   PROVERBS 29:25

FATHER OF LIES   (JOHN 8:44)

uptight   uneasy   apprehensive   misgiving   worry   stress   faltering   instability   feeble   overdo   overextended

over-fatigued   impoverished   exhausted   pretense   ambiguity   uncertainty   doubts   wavering   hypocrisy

vagueness   lies   fraud   deception   broken promises   ignorance   obtuse   disbelief   distrust   agnosticism

Face-to-Face
Creative Responses to God, Jesus, Holy Spirit

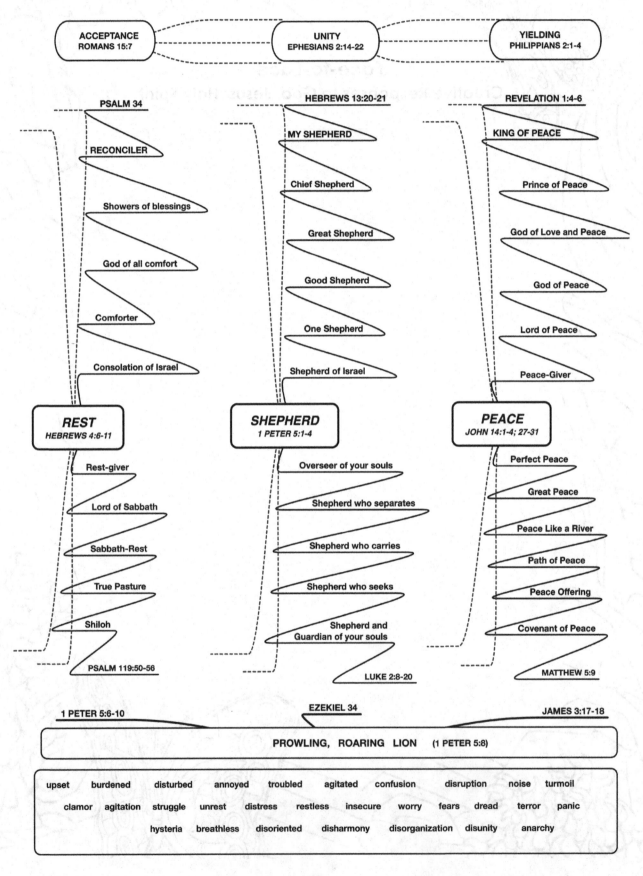

PEACEMAKER
PSALM 23

| ACCEPTANCE ROMANS 15:7 | UNITY EPHESIANS 2:14-22 | YIELDING PHILIPPIANS 2:1-4 |

PSALM 34

- RECONCILER
- Showers of blessings
- God of all comfort
- Comforter
- Consolation of Israel

HEBREWS 13:20-21

- MY SHEPHERD
- Chief Shepherd
- Great Shepherd
- Good Shepherd
- One Shepherd
- Shepherd of Israel

REVELATION 1:4-6

- KING OF PEACE
- Prince of Peace
- God of Love and Peace
- God of Peace
- Lord of Peace
- Peace-Giver

REST
HEBREWS 4:6-11

- Rest-giver
- Lord of Sabbath
- Sabbath-Rest
- True Pasture
- Shiloh

PSALM 119:50-56

SHEPHERD
1 PETER 5:1-4

- Overseer of your souls
- Shepherd who separates
- Shepherd who carries
- Shepherd who seeks
- Shepherd and Guardian of your souls

LUKE 2:8-20

PEACE
JOHN 14:1-4; 27-31

- Perfect Peace
- Great Peace
- Peace Like a River
- Path of Peace
- Peace Offering
- Covenant of Peace

MATTHEW 5:9

1 PETER 5:6-10   **EZEKIEL 34**   **JAMES 3:17-18**

PROWLING, ROARING LION (1 PETER 5:8)

upset   burdened   disturbed   annoyed   troubled   agitated   confusion   disruption   noise   turmoil

clamor   agitation   struggle   unrest   distress   restless   insecure   worry   fears   dread   terror   panic

hysteria   breathless   disoriented   disharmony   disorganization   disunity   anarchy

Peacemaker
Creative Responses to God, Jesus, Holy Spirit

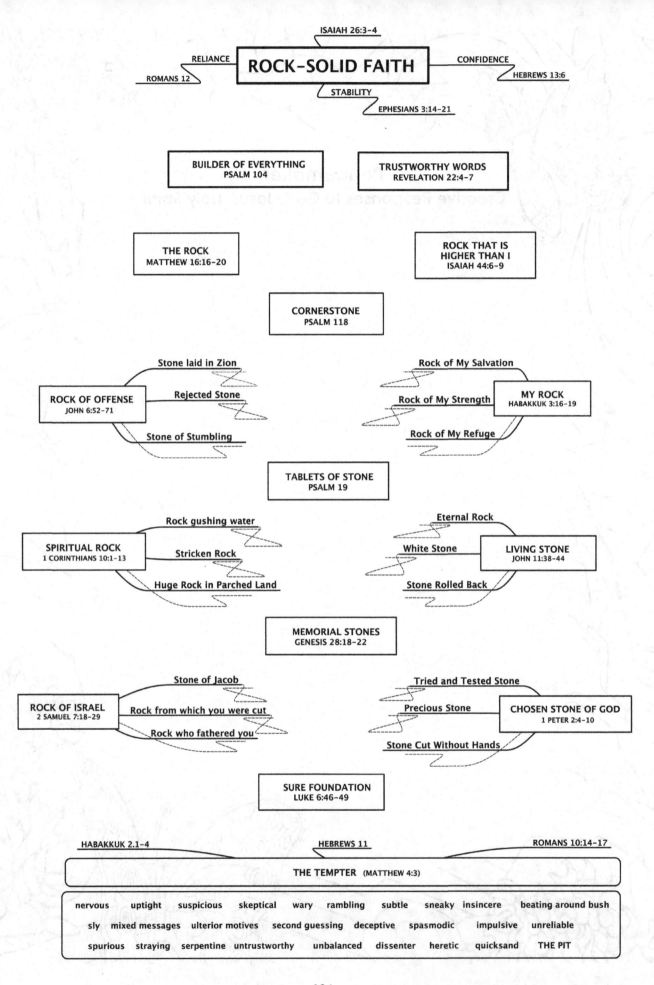

ISAIAH 26:3-4

RELIANCE

ROCK-SOLID FAITH

CONFIDENCE

ROMANS 12

HEBREWS 13:6

STABILITY

EPHESIANS 3:14-21

BUILDER OF EVERYTHING
PSALM 104

TRUSTWORTHY WORDS
REVELATION 22:4-7

THE ROCK
MATTHEW 16:16-20

ROCK THAT IS HIGHER THAN I
ISAIAH 44:6-9

CORNERSTONE
PSALM 118

Stone laid in Zion

Rock of My Salvation

ROCK OF OFFENSE
JOHN 6:52-71

Rejected Stone

Rock of My Strength

MY ROCK
HABAKKUK 3:16-19

Stone of Stumbling

Rock of My Refuge

TABLETS OF STONE
PSALM 19

Rock gushing water

Eternal Rock

SPIRITUAL ROCK
1 CORINTHIANS 10:1-13

Stricken Rock

White Stone

LIVING STONE
JOHN 11:38-44

Huge Rock in Parched Land

Stone Rolled Back

MEMORIAL STONES
GENESIS 28:18-22

Stone of Jacob

Tried and Tested Stone

ROCK OF ISRAEL
2 SAMUEL 7:18-29

Rock from which you were cut

Precious Stone

CHOSEN STONE OF GOD
1 PETER 2:4-10

Rock who fathered you

Stone Cut Without Hands

SURE FOUNDATION
LUKE 6:46-49

HABAKKUK 2.1-4

HEBREWS 11

ROMANS 10:14-17

THE TEMPTER (MATTHEW 4:3)

nervous   uptight   suspicious   skeptical   wary   rambling   subtle   sneaky   insincere   beating around bush

sly   mixed messages   ulterior motives   second guessing   deceptive   spasmodic   impulsive   unreliable

spurious   straying   serpentine   untrustworthy   unbalanced   dissenter   heretic   quicksand   THE PIT

Rock-Solid Faith
Creative Responses to God, Jesus, Holy Spirit

ROOTED IN LOVE
EPHESIANS 3:17-19

COMMITMENT
MARK 12:28-34

OBEDIENCE
JOHN 14:15-26

SELF-DENIAL
LUKE 9:23-24

FIRST LOVE

1 JOHN 4:7-12

Kindness and Love of God

God of Love and Peace

Spirit of Love

Everlasting Covenant

Keeper of Covenant Love

My Covenant

New Covenant

ROMANS 8:31-39

Covenant of the People

Covenant of Peace

Covenant of Salt

Kinsman-Redeemer

Husband

Bridegroom

Chosen One

ISAIAH 54

My Yoke

Arms

Right Hand

UNFAILING LOVE
PSALM 13

Enduring Love

Abounding Love

Great Love

Fairest of Ten Thousand

Altogether Lovely

Jealous

Faithful and True

SONG OF SOLOMON

Pure

Beloved

Kindness

Unchanging One

Spirit of Promise

Promise

Seal

JOHN 15:9-17

Bearer of Burdens

Friend of Tax Collectors, Sinners

Friend

LOVE
1 CORINTHIANS 13
1 JOHN 4:16-18

PSALM 136

JOHN 3:16-18

ROMANS 5:6-8

YOUR ENEMY, THE (D)EVIL   (1 PETER 5:8)

impatience   hurt feelings   pettiness   inconsiderate   rude   envy   frustration   offended   distrust   suspicion   fear   skepticism

defensiveness   giving up   turning away   rejection   self-indulgence   self-seeking   self-pity   self-centered   self-exaltation

self-ambition   irresponsibility   pride   indifference

Rooted in Love
Creative Responses to God, Jesus, Holy Spirit

CHAPTER 6

God's Delight: Hide-and-Seek

List of Creative Clusters

Garden of Discipleship

Hidden Treasures

Run with Perseverance

Secret of Being Content

Surprised by Joy

Carrie's Joy: Connected

(love and trust)

Carrie heard echoes of laughter. She ran the rest of the way up to the mountain peak and looked down into a valley. She couldn't believe her eyes. Children and butterflies squealed with delight as they played hide-and-seek. A wonderful sound caught her attention, and she turned to see the most beautiful waterfall in the world. Endless rainbows glistened in the middle of it. Standing close to the waterfall was the image of her Father with Joy resting on His heart. Joy wasn't shattered anymore. She was totally transformed. She had two new wings, love and trust, that moved together in perfect harmony. Carrie no longer needed to ask her question.

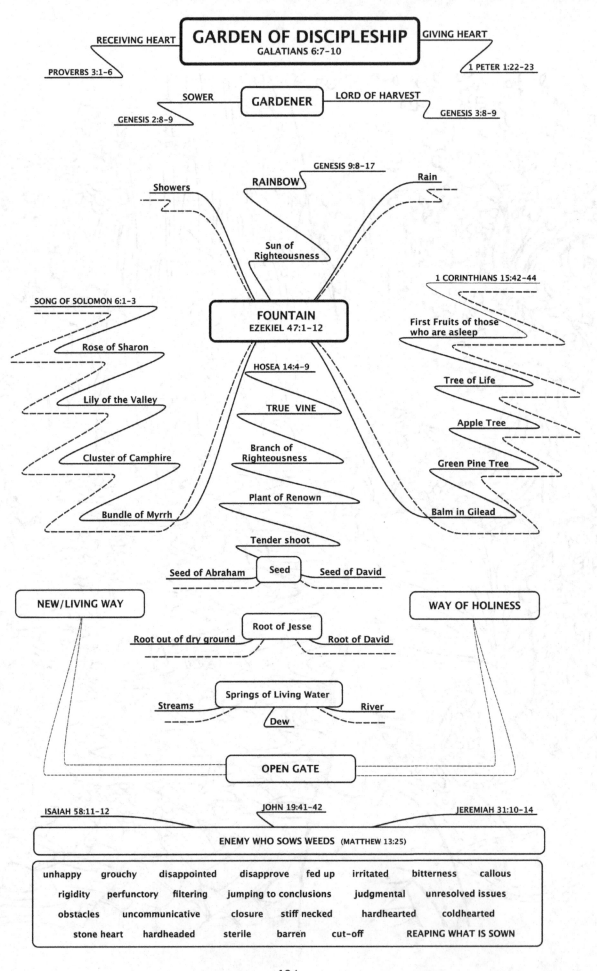

GARDEN OF DISCIPLESHIP
GALATIANS 6:7-10

RECEIVING HEART

GIVING HEART

PROVERBS 3:1-6

1 PETER 1:22-23

SOWER

GARDENER

LORD OF HARVEST

GENESIS 2:8-9

GENESIS 3:8-9

GENESIS 9:8-17

Showers

RAINBOW

Rain

Sun of
Righteousness

1 CORINTHIANS 15:42-44

SONG OF SOLOMON 6:1-3

FOUNTAIN
EZEKIEL 47:1-12

First Fruits of those
who are asleep

Rose of Sharon

HOSEA 14:4-9

Tree of Life

Lily of the Valley

TRUE VINE

Apple Tree

Branch of
Righteousness

Green Pine Tree

Cluster of Camphire

Plant of Renown

Balm in Gilead

Bundle of Myrrh

Tender shoot

Seed of Abraham

Seed

Seed of David

NEW/LIVING WAY

WAY OF HOLINESS

Root of Jesse

Root out of dry ground

Root of David

Streams

Springs of Living Water

River

Dew

OPEN GATE

ISAIAH 58:11-12

JOHN 19:41-42

JEREMIAH 31:10-14

ENEMY WHO SOWS WEEDS (MATTHEW 13:25)

unhappy   grouchy   disappointed   disapprove   fed up   irritated   bitterness   callous

rigidity   perfunctory   filtering   jumping to conclusions   judgmental   unresolved issues

obstacles   uncommunicative   closure   stiff necked   hardhearted   coldhearted

stone heart   hardheaded   sterile   barren   cut-off   REAPING WHAT IS SOWN

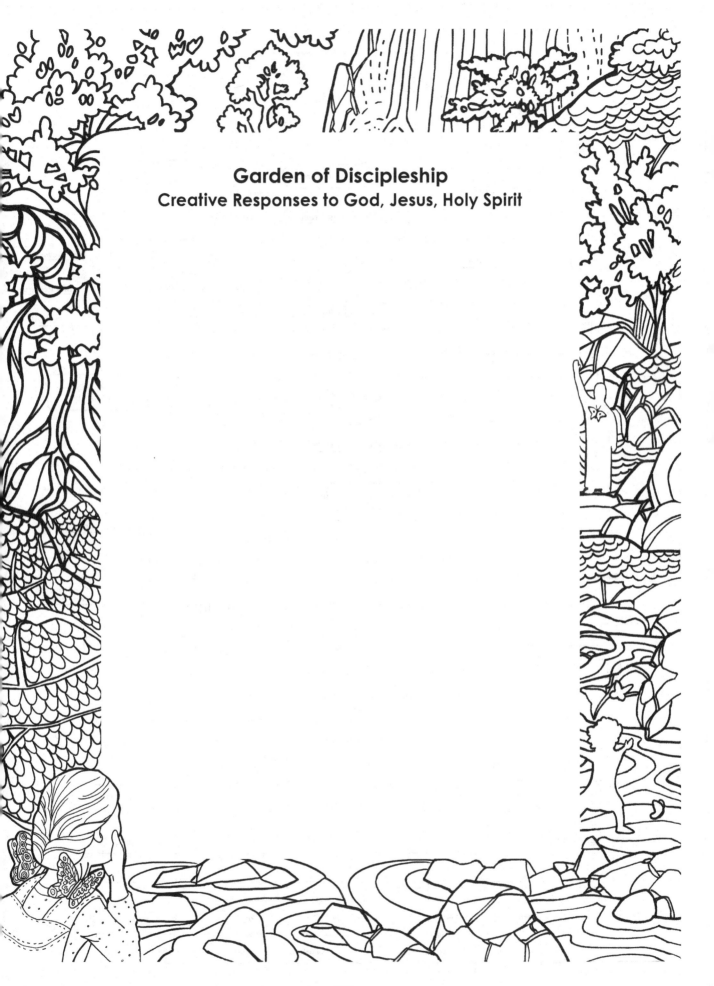

Garden of Discipleship
Creative Responses to God, Jesus, Holy Spirit

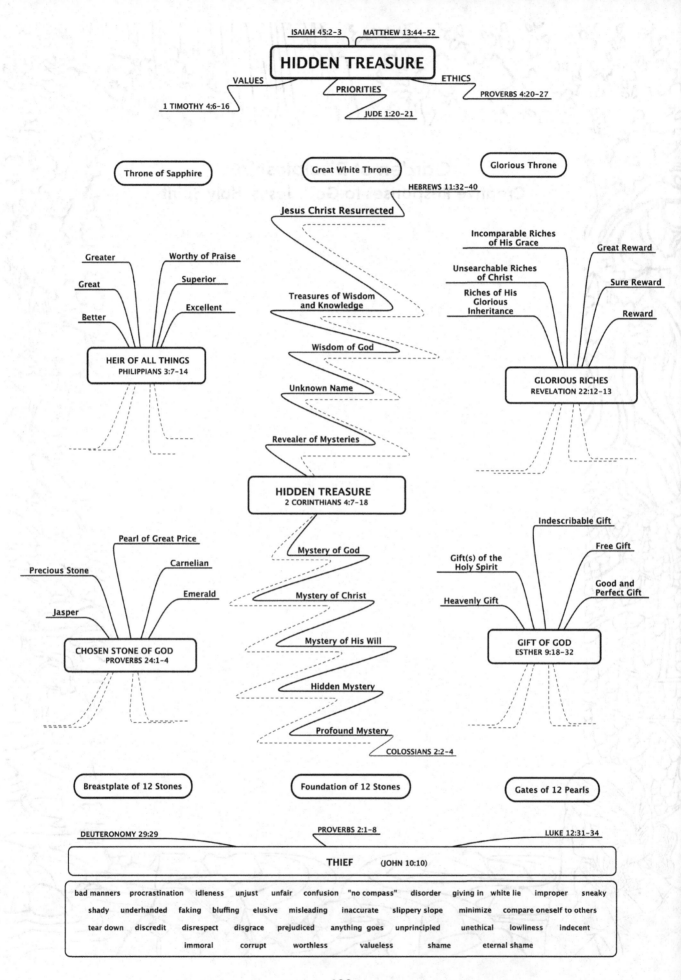

HIDDEN TREASURE

ISAIAH 45:2-3   MATTHEW 13:44-52

VALUES   PRIORITIES   ETHICS

1 TIMOTHY 4:6-16   JUDE 1:20-21   PROVERBS 4:20-27

Throne of Sapphire   Great White Throne   Glorious Throne

HEBREWS 11:32-40

Jesus Christ Resurrected

Greater   Worthy of Praise   Incomparable Riches of His Grace   Great Reward

Great   Superior   Unsearchable Riches of Christ   Sure Reward

Better   Excellent   Treasures of Wisdom and Knowledge   Riches of His Glorious Inheritance   Reward

Wisdom of God

HEIR OF ALL THINGS
PHILIPPIANS 3:7-14

Unknown Name

GLORIOUS RICHES
REVELATION 22:12-13

Revealer of Mysteries

HIDDEN TREASURE
2 CORINTHIANS 4:7-18

Indescribable Gift

Pearl of Great Price   Mystery of God   Free Gift

Precious Stone   Carnelian   Gift(s) of the Holy Spirit   Good and Perfect Gift

Emerald   Mystery of Christ

Jasper   Heavenly Gift

Mystery of His Will

CHOSEN STONE OF GOD
PROVERBS 24:1-4

Hidden Mystery

GIFT OF GOD
ESTHER 9:18-32

Profound Mystery

COLOSSIANS 2:2-4

Breastplate of 12 Stones   Foundation of 12 Stones   Gates of 12 Pearls

DEUTERONOMY 29:29   PROVERBS 2:1-8   LUKE 12:31-34

THIEF   (JOHN 10:10)

bad manners procrastination idleness unjust unfair confusion "no compass" disorder giving in white lie improper sneaky

shady underhanded faking bluffing elusive misleading inaccurate slippery slope minimize compare oneself to others

tear down discredit disrespect disgrace prejudiced anything goes unprincipled unethical lowliness indecent

immoral corrupt worthless valueless shame eternal shame

138

Hidden Treasure
Creative Responses to God, Jesus, Holy Spirit

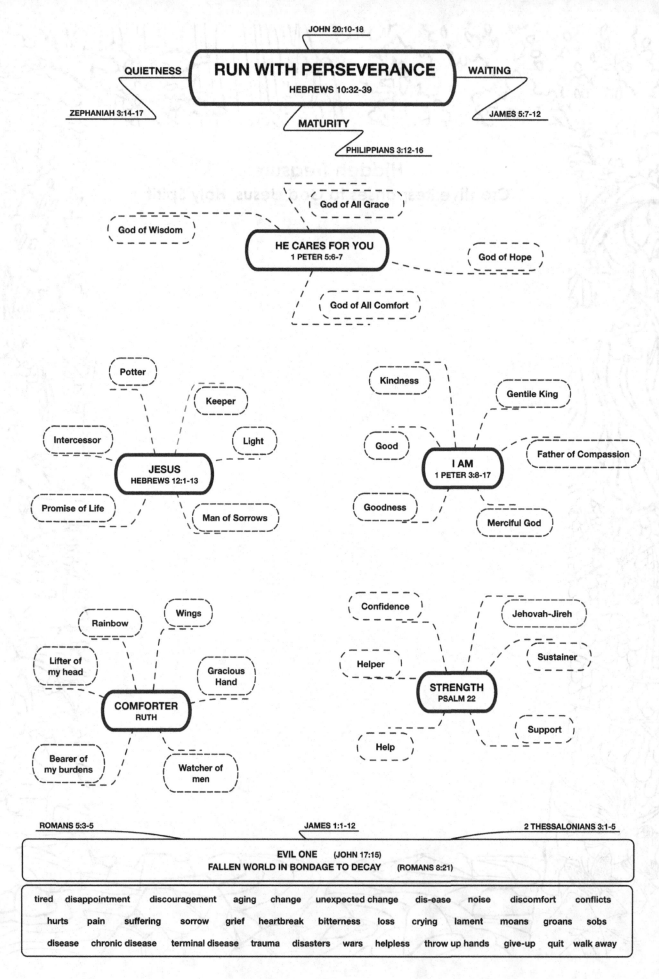

RUN WITH PERSEVERANCE
HEBREWS 10:32-39

JOHN 20:10-18

QUIETNESS
ZEPHANIAH 3:14-17

WAITING
JAMES 5:7-12

MATURITY
PHILIPPIANS 3:12-16

HE CARES FOR YOU
1 PETER 5:6-7

God of Wisdom
God of All Grace
God of Hope
God of All Comfort

JESUS
HEBREWS 12:1-13

Potter
Keeper
Light
Intercessor
Promise of Life
Man of Sorrows

I AM
1 PETER 3:8-17

Kindness
Gentile King
Good
Father of Compassion
Goodness
Merciful God

COMFORTER
RUTH

Rainbow
Wings
Lifter of my head
Gracious Hand
Bearer of my burdens
Watcher of men

STRENGTH
PSALM 22

Confidence
Jehovah-Jireh
Helper
Sustainer
Help
Support

ROMANS 5:3-5
JAMES 1:1-12
2 THESSALONIANS 3:1-5

EVIL ONE   (JOHN 17:15)
FALLEN WORLD IN BONDAGE TO DECAY   (ROMANS 8:21)

tired disappointment discouragement aging change unexpected change dis-ease noise discomfort conflicts

hurts pain suffering sorrow grief heartbreak bitterness loss crying lament moans groans sobs

disease chronic disease terminal disease trauma disasters wars helpless throw up hands give-up quit walk away

Run with Perseverance
Creative Responses to God, Jesus, Holy Spirit

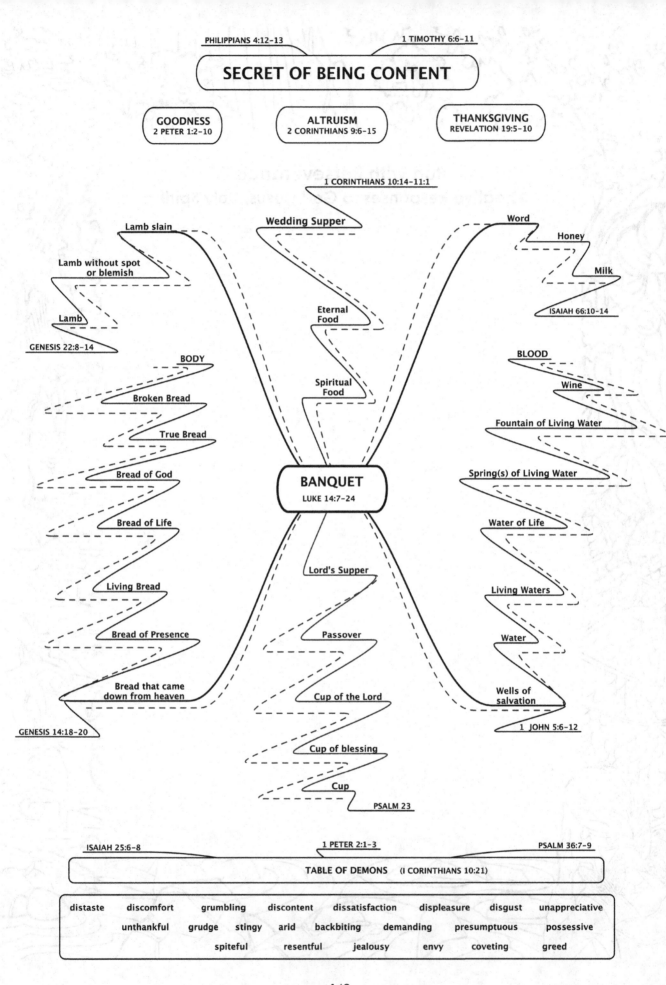

SECRET OF BEING CONTENT

PHILIPPIANS 4:12-13   1 TIMOTHY 6:6-11

GOODNESS
2 PETER 1:2-10

ALTRUISM
2 CORINTHIANS 9:6-15

THANKSGIVING
REVELATION 19:5-10

1 CORINTHIANS 10:14-11:1

Wedding Supper

Word

Honey

Milk

ISAIAH 66:10-14

Lamb slain

Lamb without spot
or blemish

Lamb

GENESIS 22:8-14

Eternal
Food

Spiritual
Food

BODY

Broken Bread

True Bread

Bread of God

Bread of Life

Living Bread

Bread of Presence

Bread that came
down from heaven

GENESIS 14:18-20

BANQUET
LUKE 14:7-24

BLOOD

Wine

Fountain of Living Water

Spring(s) of Living Water

Water of Life

Living Waters

Water

Wells of
salvation

1 JOHN 5:6-12

Lord's Supper

Passover

Cup of the Lord

Cup of blessing

Cup

PSALM 23

ISAIAH 25:6-8   1 PETER 2:1-3   PSALM 36:7-9

TABLE OF DEMONS   (I CORINTHIANS 10:21)

distaste	discomfort	grumbling	discontent	dissatisfaction	displeasure	disgust	unappreciative
unthankful	grudge	stingy	arid	backbiting	demanding	presumptuous	possessive
	spiteful	resentful	jealousy	envy	coveting	greed	

Secret of Being Content
Creative Responses to God, Jesus, Holy Spirit

SURPRISED BY JOY

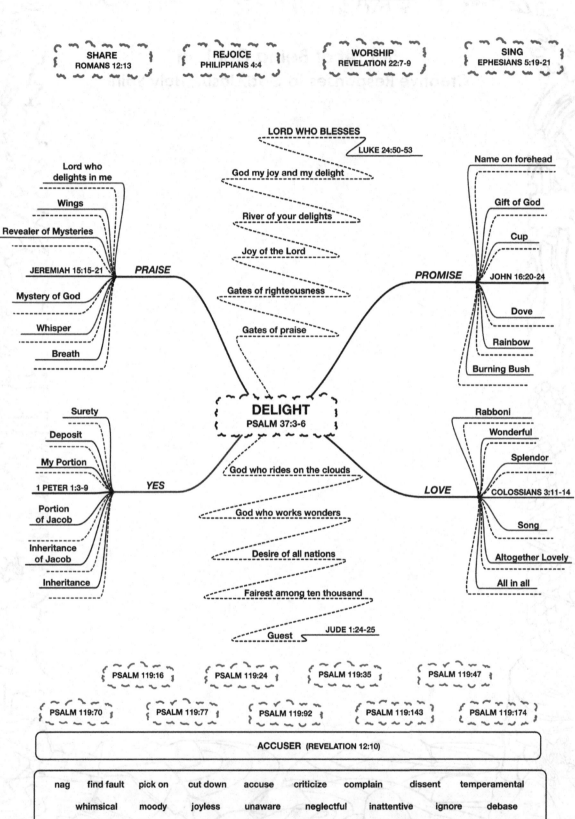

SHARE
ROMANS 12:13

REJOICE
PHILIPPIANS 4:4

WORSHIP
REVELATION 22:7-9

SING
EPHESIANS 5:19-21

LORD WHO BLESSES
LUKE 24:50-53

God my joy and my delight

River of your delights

Joy of the Lord

Gates of righteousness

Gates of praise

Lord who delights in me

Wings

Revealer of Mysteries

JEREMIAH 15:15-21   *PRAISE*

Mystery of God

Whisper

Breath

Name on forehead

Gift of God

Cup

PROMISE   JOHN 16:20-24

Dove

Rainbow

Burning Bush

DELIGHT
PSALM 37:3-6

Surety

Deposit

My Portion

1 PETER 1:3-9   *YES*

Portion of Jacob

Inheritance of Jacob

Inheritance

God who rides on the clouds

God who works wonders

Desire of all nations

Fairest among ten thousand

Guest   JUDE 1:24-25

Rabboni

Wonderful

Splendor

LOVE   COLOSSIANS 3:11-14

Song

Altogether Lovely

All in all

PSALM 119:16   PSALM 119:24   PSALM 119:35   PSALM 119:47

PSALM 119:70   PSALM 119:77   PSALM 119:92   PSALM 119:143   PSALM 119:174

ACCUSER (REVELATION 12:10)

nag	find fault	pick on	cut down	accuse	criticize	complain	dissent	temperamental
whimsical	moody	joyless	unaware	neglectful	inattentive	ignore	debase
	hate	curse	profane	desecrate			

Surprised by Joy
Creative Responses to God, Jesus, Holy Spirit

EPILOGUE

Carrie's Joy: Transformed

(delight)

Carrie played hide-and-seek with Joy, Freedom, and Grace—and talked with her Father—all to her heart's content. She promised Him that she would continue to care deeply and reach out to others in His name, no matter what happened. By persevering in "That Way," she knew she would help her Father crush the biggest bully of all time.[33] As she started to leave, He placed a small box in her hands and whispered, "This is to light your path on the way home." She could hardly wait to open it. Without a doubt, it was full of *de-light*!

That Way [34]
Someone came
And let me hurt,
Let me talk,
Let me laugh,
And let me cry.
Let me be me,
And loved me
THAT WAY
I saw Love
And Trust
Soar on Wings

---

[33] Romans 16:20
[34] Janice R. S. Looper, 1999. Adapted and used with permission.

Section 4

Seek and Delight in Him

Ask and it will be given to you;

seek and you will find;

knock and the door will be opened to you.

For everyone who asks receives;

he who seeks finds;

and to him who knocks the door will be opened.

Matthew 7:7–8

Permission to Be Different and Incomplete

My passionate goal to color God's names, attributes, images, and descriptions in multiple Bibles over the past twenty-five years has expanded my alphabetical list to over eight hundred names. But two annoying convictions frequently hindered my journey. I erroneously believed that all the lists of His names had to be identical and all-inclusive. To overcome this obstacle, the God of all grace sent two experienced pilgrims to safeguard my sanity. Scholar James Large emphasized that no two Bible students could arrive at exact results while compiling a catalog of this nature.[35] Dr. Herbert Lockyer believed that it would be next to impossible to classify all of God's names and that such a project would be a mind-staggering task.[36] Freed from my burden of perfectionism, I accepted the reality that my personal alphabetical list will remain different and incomplete on this side of heaven.

One of these differences offers the possibility to unpack some of His names. For example: instead of just *shepherd*, there are eleven descriptions of *shepherd*; instead of just *stone*, there are twelve descriptions of *stone*; instead of one *throne*, there are twenty descriptions of *throne*. The variety of adjectives and descriptions comprises an infinite array of colors and musical notes that add three-dimensional depth to meditation, prayer, and worship. A second difference is that I place most adjectives and descriptions after His names. For example, you will not find *everlasting Father* or *righteous Father*, but *Father, everlasting* and *Father, righteous*. This helps identify similar names and locate them quickly for clustering. The list remains most incomplete concerning the vast descriptions of *God who, Lord who, He who, One who*. God's essence as I AM truly staggers the mind.

His all-encompassing nature also reveals the limits of space. Selecting Scripture references to use for each name proved exceptionally challenging. I set a goal to provide at least the first (seed), middle (plant), and last references (flower or fruit). I am indebted to Dr. Stewart Custer of Bob Jones University for teaching me the invaluable concept of tracing the seeds, plants, and fruits of biblical themes. Dr. A. T. Pierson calls this same concept "the Law of First Mention."[37] Please be aware that some names like *God, Lord,* and *Lord God* have over a thousand references in an exhaustive concordance. Therefore I made no attempt to reflect the frequency of usage. Other names like *Author of Life, Dew, Fullness of Deity, Profound Mystery, God of hope, God of all grace, God of all comfort, Lion of Judah,* and *Unknown name* appear only once or twice in Scripture. Fewer references don't diminish the relevance of a name. If anything, they are like unique pearls to be cherished. I pray that God blesses your adventure while using this list and that you will truly delight in Him!

---

[35] James Large, *Titles & Symbols of Christ* (Chattanooga: AMG Publishers, 1994), xi.

[36] Lockyer, 86–87, 90.

[37] Ibid., 5.

Alphabetical List of Names

Attributes, Descriptions, Images, Metaphors, Prototypes

A

Abba (Mark 14:36; Romans 8:15; Galatians 4:6)

Adam, one, last, second man (Romans 5:14, 5:19; 1 Corinthians 15:21–22, 15:45–47)

Advocate (intercedes) (Job 16:19; Romans 8:26–27, 8:34; Hebrews 7:25; 1 John 2:1)

Alien (Psalm 69:8; Isaiah 28:21)

All in all (Colossians 3:11)

Almighty, the (Genesis 17:1; Exodus 6:3; Ruth 1:20–21; Job 37:23; Psalm 91:1; Revelation 1:8, 4:8, 11:17, 15:3, 16:7, 16:14, 19:6, 19:15, and 21:22)

Alpha and Omega (Revelation 1:8, 21:6, and 22:13)

Altar (Genesis 8:20, 22:9–13; Exodus 29:36–30:10; Psalm 43:4; Hebrews 13:10; Revelation 16:7)

Altogether lovely (Song of Solomon 5:16)

Amen (2 Corinthians 1:20; Revelation 3:14)

Anchor for the soul (Hebrews 6:18–20)

Ancient of days (Daniel 7:9, 7:13, and 7:22)

Angel of God (Genesis 16:7–12, 21:17–18, 22:11–18, 31:11–13, and 48:16; Exodus 3:2–4, 14:19, and 23:20–23; Psalm 34:7)

Angel of His presence (Exodus 33:14; Isaiah 63:9)

Anointed One (Psalms 2:2, 45:7; Isaiah 61:1; Daniel 9:25–26; Luke 4:18; John 1:41; Acts 4:26, 10:38)

Apostle (Hebrews 3:1)

Architect (Hebrews 11:10)

Ark of the covenant (Exodus 25:10–16; Numbers 7:89, 10:33–36; Joshua 3:3–4; 2 Samuel 6; 1 Kings 8:1–11; Hebrews 9:4–5; Revelation 11:19)

Arm(s) (Exodus 6:6; Numbers 11:23; Psalms 89:13, 98:1; Isaiah 40:10–11, 53:1; Mark 9:36, 10:16; Luke 1:51–52; John 12:38)

Arm(s), everlasting (Deuteronomy 33:27)

Armor of God (light) (Romans 13:12; Ephesians 6:11–13)

Arrow, polished (Psalm 45:5; Isaiah 49:2)

Author (prince) of life (Acts 3:15)

Author (perfecter, finisher) of our faith (Hebrews 12:2)

Author (source) of eternal salvation (Hebrews 2:10, 5:9)

B

Baby of Bethlehem (Luke 2:8–16)

Balm in Gilead (Jeremiah 8:22)

Banner (Exodus 17:15; Psalm 60:4; Song of Solomon 2:4; Isaiah 11:10, 49:22, and 62:10)

Banquet (wedding) (Song of Solomon 2:4; Isaiah 25:6–8; Matthew 22:1–14; Luke 14:15–24; Revelation 19:7–9)

Bearer of burdens (Psalms 68:19, 81:6; Isaiah 53:4; Matthew 11:28–30)

Bearer of sins (Isaiah 53:11; 1 Corinthians 15:3; Hebrews 9:28; 1 Peter 2:24)

Beginning and End (Revelation 21:6; 22:13)

Beloved (loved one) (Song of Solomon 2:16, 5, and 7:10; Matthew 3:17; Mark 12:6; Ephesians 1:6)

Better (Psalms 63:3, 84:10, and 118:8–9; Luke 10:42; Philippians 1:23; Hebrews 11:40)

Blessings, everlasting (1 Chronicles 17:27; Psalms 21:6, 45:2, and 133:3)

Blessings, showers of (Psalm 72:6; Ezekiel 34:26–27; Hosea 10:12; Malachi 3:10–12)

Blood, poured out (Matthew 26:27–29; Mark 14:23–25; Luke 22:20; John 6:53–57; 1 Corinthians 11:25–29)

Body, given (Matthew 26:26; Mark 14:22; Luke 22:19; John 19:31–34; 1 Corinthians 11:23–24)

Book of life (Exodus 32:32; Psalm 69:28; Luke 10:20; Philippians 4:3; Hebrews 12:23; Revelation 3:5, 17:8, 20:12, and 21:27)

Book of the law (Moses) (Deuteronomy 31:24–26; Nehemiah 8; Matthew 5:17–20)

Branch (of righteousness) (Isaiah 4:2, 11:1; Jeremiah 23:5, 33:15; Zechariah 3:8, 6:12)

Bread of God (John 6:33)

Bread of life (John 6:35, 48–51)

Bread of presence (Exodus 25:30, 35:13; Leviticus 24:5–8; Numbers 4:7; 1 Samuel 21:3–6; Matthew 12:1–8)

Bread that came down from heaven (manna) (John 6:33, 6:41, 6:50–51, and 6:58)

Bread, broken (Matthew 26:26; Mark 14:22; Luke 22:19, 24:30, and 24:35; 1 Corinthians 11:23–24)

Bread, living (John 6:51)

Bread, true (John 6:32)

Breastplate of twelve stones (Exodus 28:15–30; Leviticus 8:8)

Breastplate of righteousness (Isaiah 59:17)

Breath (of God) (Job 27:3, 33:4; Psalm 33:6; Ezekiel 37:5–10; Luke 23:46; John 20:22; Acts 17:25; 2 Thessalonians 2:8; 2 Timothy 3:16–17)

Breath of life (Genesis 1:30, 2:7, 6:17, and 7:15; Revelation 11:11–12)

Bridegroom (Psalm 45; Song of Solomon; Isaiah 61:10, 62:4–5; Hosea 2:19–20; Matthew 9:15, 25:1–13; John 3:29; Revelation 19:6–9, 21:1–3)

Brother (elder) (Matthew 12:50; Mark 3:35; Romans 8:29; Hebrews 2:11–12)

Builder of everything (Hebrews 3:4, 11:10)

Bush, burning (Exodus 3:2–5; Acts 7:30–32)

C

Camphire, cluster of (henna) (Song of Solomon 1:14)

Captain of our salvation (KJV) (Hebrews 2:10)

Carnelian (Revelation 4:3)

Carpenter (Matthew 13:55; Mark 6:3)

Child (Isaiah 9:6; Luke 2:21–39)

Chosen one (elect) (Isaiah 42:1; Matthew 12:18; Luke 9:35, 23:35, 1 Peter 2:4, 2:6)

Christ (Matthew 1:16, 16:16; Luke 24:26; Acts 17:3; Romans 5:6–8; Galatians 3:26–29; Philippians 3:7–11; Hebrews 10:5–7; 1 Peter 3:18; Revelation 20:4, 20:6)

Christ Jesus (Acts 24:24; Romans 6:3, 8:34; 1 Corinthians 1:4, 1:30; Galatians 5:24; Ephesians 2:13, 2:20; Philippians 2:5; 1 Timothy 1:1; 2 Timothy 2:1; Philemon 1:1)

Christ Jesus (the) our Lord (Luke 2:11; Acts 2:36; Romans 6:23, 8:39; 1 Corinthians 15:31; Ephesians 3:10–11; Colossians 2:6; 1 Timothy 1:2, 1:12; 2 Timothy 1:2)

Christ Jesus our Savior (Titus 1:4)

Christ who is God over all forever praised (Romans 9:5)

City of refuge (Numbers 35)

Comforter (Psalms 23:1–4, 86:17, and 119:76; Isaiah 51:3, 51:12, 52:9, 57:18, 61:1–2, and 66:13; Jeremiah 8:18, 31:13; Zechariah 1:17; 2 Corinthians 7:6; Philippians 2:1–2)

Comforter, another (KJV) (John 14:16, 14:26, and 15:26; Acts 9:31; 2 Corinthians 1:4)

Commander at (of) sea (Exodus 14:21–28; Job 26:12; Psalms 74:13, 107:29; Isaiah 50:2; Matthew 14:25–33; Mark 4:39–41; Hebrews 11:29; Revelation 20:13)

Commander of the Lord's army (Joshua 5:14–15)

Confidence (Psalm 71:5; Proverbs 3:26)

Consolation of Israel (Luke 2:25)

Cornerstone (Psalm 118:22; Isaiah 28:16; Zechariah 10:4; Matthew 21:42; Luke

20:17–18; Acts 4:11; Ephesians 2:20;
1 Peter 2:6)

Counselor (Psalm 16:7; Isaiah 9:6, 28:29; John
14:25, 15:26, and 16:7; Romans 11:33–34)

Covenant of peace (Isaiah 54:10; Ezekiel 34:25,
37:26; Malachi 2:5)

Covenant of salt (Leviticus 2:13; Numbers
18:19; 2 Chronicles 13:5; Colossians 4:6)

Covenant of the people (Isaiah 42:6, 49:8;
Jeremiah 31:31–33)

Covenant, everlasting (Genesis 9:16, 17:7, 17:13,
and 17:19; 2 Samuel 23:5; Psalm 105:8–10;
Isaiah 55:3, 61:8; Jeremiah 32:40, 50:5;
Ezekiel 37:26; Hebrews 13:20)

Covenant, My (Genesis 6:18, 9:9–17, 17:2–7,
and 17:10–14; Deuteronomy 5:2, 31:20;
Hosea 8:1; Zechariah 9:11; Matthew 26:28;
Romans 11:27)

Covenant, new (Jeremiah 31:31; Luke 22:20;
1 Corinthians 11:25; 2 Corinthians 3:6;
Hebrews 8:10–13, 12:22–24)

Creator (Genesis 1, 14:19, and 14:22; Ecclesiastes
12:1; Isaiah 40:28; Romans 1:25; Ephesians
3:9; Colossians 1:16, 3:10; Hebrews 1:2;
1 Peter 4:19; Revelation 4:11)

Cross of our Lord Jesus Christ (John 19:17;
Acts 2:23; 1 Corinthians 1:17; Galatians
6:12; Ephesians 2:16; Philippians 2:8;
Colossians 1:20, 2:14–15; Hebrews 12:2)

Cross, message of the (1 Corinthians 1:18)

Cross, offense of the (Galatians 3:13, 5:11)

Crown of glory (Isaiah 28:5, 62:3; Hebrews 2:9;
1 Peter 5:4)

Crown of life (James 1:12; Revelation 2:10)

Crown of thorns (Matthew 27:29; Mark 15:17;
John 19:2)

Crowns, many (Revelation 19:12)

Cup (Psalms 16:5, 116:13; Luke 22:17, 20)

Cup of blessing (thanksgiving) (1 Corinthians
10:16)

Cup of the Lord (1 Corinthians 10:21)

Curtain, torn (Exodus 26:31–33, 40:21;
Leviticus 16:2; Matthew 27:51; Mark 15:38;
Luke 23:45; Hebrews 6:19, 10:19–20)

D

Dawn (dayspring) (Job 38:12–13; Isaiah 9:2,
58:8; Matthew 4:16, 28:1)

Day of atonement (Leviticus 16; Hebrews
9:24–25)

Defender (defense) (Job 19:25; Proverbs 23:11;
Isaiah 51:22)

Defender of widows (Deuteronomy 10:18;
Psalm 68:5)

Delight (1 Samuel 2:1; Nehemiah 1:11; Psalms
35:9, 37:4, and 43:4; Proverbs 8:30; Song of
Solomon 1:4, 2:3; Isaiah 61:10)

Deliverer (2 Samuel 22:2; Psalms 18:2, 34:4,
34:7, 34:17, 34:19, 37:40, 40:17, 70:5, 140:7,
and 144:2; Romans 11:26)

Deposit (2 Corinthians 1:22, 5:5; Ephesians 1:14;
2 Timothy 1:14)

Desire of all the nations (Haggai 2:7)

Dew (Hosea 14:5)

Door (Hosea 2:15; Matthew 7:7–8, 25:10;
Luke 11:9–10, 13:22–25; John 10:7–9;
Revelation 3:8)

Dove (Genesis 8:8–12; Matthew 3:16; Mark 1:10;
Luke 3:22; John 1:32)

Dwelling place (Leviticus 26:11; Psalms 27:4–5,
90:1, and 91:1; John 14:1–3; 2 Corinthians
5:2–4; Revelation 21:3)

E

Emerald (Revelation 4:3)

Encouragement (eternal) (Romans 15:5;
2 Thessalonians 2:16)

Everlasting to everlasting (1 Chronicles 16:36,
29:10; Nehemiah 9:5; Psalms 41:13, 90:2,
103:17, and 106:48)

Excellent (Psalm 45:2; 1 Corinthians 12:31)

F

Face of God (Christ) (Genesis 32:30; Exodus
33:11, 33:20; Numbers 6:25–26;
Deuteronomy 5:4, 34:10; Psalms 27:8,
44:3, 105:4, and 119:58; Matthew 17:2;

1 Corinthians 13:12; 2 Corinthians 4:6; Revelation 1:16, 22:4)

Fairest (outstanding) of ten thousand (Song of Solomon 5:10)

Faithful and true (1 Thessalonians 5:24; Revelation 19:11)

Father (Isaiah 1:2; Jeremiah 3:19; Hosea 11:1; Malachi 1:6; Matthew 11:25–27, 28:19; John 1:14, 6:44–46, and 14:1–31; Ephesians 4:6; Hebrews 1:5; 1 John 3:1; Revelation 14:1)

Father in heaven, heavenly (Matthew 5:45, 5:48, 6:1, 6:9, 6:14, 6:26, 6:32, 7:11, 12:50, 15:13, 16:17, 18:10, and 18:19; Mark 11:25; Luke 11:13)

Father of compassion (Psalm 103:13; Malachi 3:17; 2 Corinthians 1:3)

Father of glory (John 12:28, 15:8; Ephesians 1:17)

Father of heavenly lights (James 1:17)

Father of Israel (Exodus 4:22; Deuteronomy 32:6; Isaiah 1:2; Jeremiah 31:9)

Father of orphans (of fatherless) (Psalms 27:10, 68:5, and 146:9; John 14:18)

Father of prodigal (Luke 15:11–24)

Father of Solomon (2 Samuel 7:14; 1 Chronicles 22:10, 28:6)

Father who sees (Matthew 6:4, 6:6, and 6:18)

Father who sent (Matthew 10:40; John 3:16–17, 5:36–38, 6:38–40, 8:18, 8:42, 12:44–50, and 20:21; Romans 8:3; 1 John 4:14)

Father, everlasting (Isaiah 9:6)

Father, holy (Matthew 6:9; Luke 11:2; John 17:11)

Father, living (John 5:26, 6:57)

Father, loving (Hosea 11:1–4; John 3:16–17, 3:35, 5:20, 10:17, 14:21, 14:23, 15:9, 16:27, and 17:23–26; 1 John 3:1, 4:9–10)

Father, merciful (Luke 6:36)

Father, my (Psalm 89:26; Jeremiah 3:4; Matthew 10:32–33, 26:53; Luke 2:49, 24:49; John 2:16, 20:17; Revelation 3:5, 3:21)

Father, one (only) (Malachi 2:10; Matthew 23:9; 1 Corinthians 8:6; Ephesians 4:6)

Father, our (Isaiah 63:16, 64:8; Matthew 6:9)

Father, perfect (Matthew 5:48)

Father, righteous (John 17:25)

Father, your (Deuteronomy 32:6; Matthew 5:16, 5:45, 6, and 18:14; Mark 11:25; Luke 6:36, 11:13, and 12:30–32; John 20:17; Hebrews 1:5)

Favor of God (Genesis 4:4, 6:8; Exodus 32:11, 33:12–13; Leviticus 26:9; Deuteronomy 33:16; Psalm 30:5; Proverbs 8:35; Isaiah 49:8; 61:2; Luke 1:25, 1:30, 2:14, and 4:19; 2 Corinthians 6:2)

Fear of Isaac (Genesis 31:42, 31:53)

Finger of God (Exodus 8:19, 31:18; Psalm 8:3; Mark 7:33; Luke 11:20; John 8:6)

Fire (Leviticus 9:24; Deuteronomy 5:26; Judges 6:21; 1 Chronicles 21:26; 2 Chronicles 7:1–3; Isaiah 10:17; Matthew 3:11–12; Revelation 20:14–15)

Fire, consuming (Exodus 19:18, 24:17; Deuteronomy 4:24, 9:3; 1 Kings 18:24, 18:38; 2 Kings 1:9–15; 2 Thessalonians 1:7; Hebrews 12:29)

Fire, refiner's (Psalms 12:6, 66:10; Isaiah 48:10; Zechariah 13:9; Malachi 3:2–4; 1 Peter 1:6–7)

First and last (Isaiah 41:4, 44:6, and 48:12; Revelation 1:17, 22:13)

Firstborn (Psalm 89:27; Luke 2:7; Hebrews 1:6)

Firstborn among many brothers (Romans 8:29)

Firstborn from the dead (Acts 26:23; Colossians 1:18; Revelation 1:5)

Firstborn over all creation (Colossians 1:15)

First fruits of those asleep (1 Corinthians 15:20–23)

Food, eternal (John 6:27)

Food, spiritual (true, real) (John 6:55; 1 Corinthians 10:3–5)

Forerunner (John 14:1–4; Hebrews 6:20)

Fortress (2 Samuel 22:2; Psalms 18:2, 28:8, 31:2–3, 48:3, 59:16–17, 62:2, 62:6, 71:3, 91:2, 94:22, and 144:2; Proverbs 14:26; Isaiah 17:10; Jeremiah 16:19; Zechariah 9:12)

Foundation (sure) (Isaiah 28:16, 33:6; 1 Corinthians 3:11; 2 Timothy 2:19)

Foundation of (twelve) stones (Isaiah 54:11–12; Hebrews 11:10; Revelation 21:14, 21:19–20)

Fountain (Joel 3:18; Zechariah 13:1)

Fountain of life (Psalm 36:9; Proverbs 14:27)

Fountain (spring) of living waters (Jeremiah 2:13; 17:13)

Friend (Exodus 33:11; Proverbs 17:17; Isaiah 41:8; Luke 12:4; John 11:11, 15:15; James 2:23)

Friend of tax collectors and sinners (Matthew 9:11, 11:19; Luke 7:34)

Fullness (John 1:16, Colossians 1:19)

Fullness of the Deity (Colossians 2:9)

G

Gardener (Genesis 2:8; Isaiah 27:2–3; John 15:1)

Garments of salvation (Genesis 3:21; Exodus 28:2–5; Ruth 3:9; 2 Chronicles 6:41; Psalm 22:18; Isaiah 61:10, 63:1–3; Luke 2:7, 23:53, and 24:12; John 19:24; Galatians 3:27)

Gate, narrow (Matthew 7:13–14)

Gate(s), open (Psalm 122:1–2; Isaiah 60:11, 62:10; John 10:1–10; Revelation 21:25)

Gates of twelve pearls (Revelation 21:12–13, 21:21)

Gates of praise (Psalm 100; Isaiah 60:18)

Gates of righteousness (Psalm 118:19–21; Isaiah 26:2; Revelation 22:14)

Gift of God (John 4:10; Acts 1:4; Romans 5:15–17, 6:23; 1 Corinthians 7:7; Ephesians 2:8, 3:7; 2 Timothy 1:6; 1 John 3:24)

Gift, free (Revelation 22:17)

Gift, good and perfect (James 1:17)

Gift, heavenly (Hebrews 6:4–6)

Gift, indescribable (2 Corinthians 9:15)

Gift(s) of the Holy Spirit (Luke 11:13; Acts 2:38, 10:45, and 11:17; Romans 1:11, 11:29; 1 Corinthians 12–14; Ephesians 4:7–8; 1 Timothy 4:14; Hebrews 2:4; 1 Peter 4:10)

Glory (Exodus 15:11, 40:34; 1 Kings 8:10–11; Psalms 19:1, 29:2; Isaiah 6:3; Ezekiel 10:18; Luke 2:9, 2:14; John 1:14; Hebrews 9:5; 2 Peter 1:3; Revelation 19:1, 21:23)

Glory of Israel (1 Samuel 4:21–22, 15:29; Jeremiah 2:11; Zechariah 2:5; Luke 2:32)

Glory, eternal (2 Corinthians 4:17; 2 Timothy 2:10; 1 Peter 5:10)

Glory, majestic (2 Peter 1:17)

God (Genesis 1; Psalm 68; Isaiah 40:3; Revelation 21:7, 22:9, and 22:18–19)

God Almighty (Genesis 17:1, 28:3, 35:11, 43:14, and 48:3; Exodus 6:3; Revelation 16:14)

God full of compassion (Psalm 116:5; Mark 1:41; Luke 15:20; James 5:11)

God manifest in the flesh (1 Timothy 3:16)

God Most High (Genesis 14:18–22; Psalms 7:10, 57:2, and 78:35; Daniel 3:26, 4:2, 5:18, and 5:21; Mark 5:7; Luke 8:28; Acts 16:17; Hebrews 7:1)

God my joy and my delight (*my exceeding joy in KJV*) (Psalm 43:4)

God of Abraham (Genesis 24:12, 26:24, 31:42, and 32:9; Psalm 47:9)

God of Abraham, Isaac, Jacob (Exodus 3:15–16, 4:5; 1 Kings 18:36; 1 Chronicles 29:18; Matthew 22:31–33; Acts 3:12–13, 7:32)

God of all comfort (2 Corinthians 1:3–4)

God of all grace (1 Peter 5:10)

God of Bethel (Genesis 31:13)

God of compassion (Exodus 33:19; Deuteronomy 13:17, 30:3; Judges 2:18; Psalms 119:77, 145:9; Isaiah 30:18, 54:8, and 54:10; Micah 7:19; Zechariah 10:6; Matthew 9:36, 14:14, 15:32, and 20:34; Romans 9:15)

God of compassion, great (deep) (Nehemiah 9:19, 9:27; Psalms 51:1, 119:156; Isaiah 54:7; Jeremiah 31:20)

God of Daniel (Daniel 6:16–27)

God of David (2 Kings 20:5; 2 Chronicles 21:12; Isaiah 38:5)

God of Elijah (2 Kings 2:14)

God of Gentiles (Romans 3:29)

God of glory (Psalms 19:1, 29:3; Proverbs 25:2; Isaiah 60:19; John 11:40; Acts 7:2; 2 Corinthians 4:6; Revelation 21:23)

God of gods (greater than) (Exodus 18:11; Deuteronomy 10:17; 2 Chronicles 2:5; Psalms 135:5, 136:2; Daniel 2:47, 11:36)

God of heaven (Genesis 24:3, 24:7; Deuteronomy 4:39; Nehemiah 1:4–5; Psalm 136:26; Daniel 2:17–19, Jonah 1:9; Revelation 11:13, 16:11)

God of Hezekiah (2 Chronicles 32:17)

God of hope (Romans 15:13)

God of Isaac (Genesis 28:13, 46:1; Exodus 4:5; 1 Chronicles 29:18)

God of Israel (Genesis 33:20; Exodus 5:1, 24:10, and 32:27; Psalm 68:35; Isaiah 45:3; Jeremiah 11:3; Matthew 15:31; Luke 1:68; Acts 13:17)

God of Jacob (2 Samuel 23:1; Psalms 20:1, 46:7, 75:9, 76:6, and 146:5; Isaiah 2:3; Micah 4:2; Acts 7:46)

God of Jerusalem (Zion) (2 Chronicles 6:6, 32:19–20; Ezra 1:3, 7:19; Psalm 135:21; Joel 3:17; Zephaniah 3:14–17; Matthew 21:5; Luke 13:34; Revelation 21)

God of justice (Deuteronomy 10:17–18; Psalms 9:16, 36:6; Isaiah 5:16, 30:18, and 61:8; Malachi 2:17; Luke 18:7; Romans 3:23–26)

God of love and peace (2 Corinthians 13:11)

God of my life (Job 33:4–7; Psalm 42:8)

God of my salvation (God who saves me) (Exodus 15:2; Psalm 51:14; Luke 2:30)

God of Nahor (Genesis 31:53)

God of patience (slow to anger) (Exodus 34:6; Numbers 14:18; Psalms 86:15, 103:8, and 145:8; Joel 2:13; Romans 2:4; 9:22; 1 Timothy 1:16; 1 Peter 3:20; 2 Peter 3:9, 3:15)

God of peace (Romans 15:33, 16:20; 1 Corinthians 14:33; Philippians 4:9; 1 Thessalonians 5:23; Hebrews 13:20)

God of Shadrach, Meshach, Abednego (Daniel 3:28–29)

God of Shem (Genesis 9:26)

God of the armies (of Israel) (1 Samuel 17:45; Isaiah 13:4; Joel 2:11; Matthew 22:7)

God of the Hebrews (Exodus 3:18, 5:3, 7:16, 9:1, 9:13, and 10:3)

God of the spirits of all flesh (mankind) (Numbers 16:22, 27:16; Jeremiah 32:27)

God of the spirits of the prophets (Revelation 22:6)

God of truth (Psalm 31:5; Isaiah 45:19, 65:16; John 3:33)

God of wisdom (Job 38–42:6; Psalm 104:24; Proverbs 1–9; Isaiah 28:29; Jeremiah 10:12; Daniel 2:20–23; Luke 2:52; Romans 16:27; Ephesians 3:10; James 3:17; Revelation 5:12)

God of your (my) father(s) (Genesis 31:5, 43:23, and 46:3; Exodus 3:6; Deuteronomy 1:21, 27:3; Acts 3:13, 5:30, 7:32, 22:14, and 24:14)

God our (my) Savior (1 Chronicles 16:35; Psalms 18:46, 65:5, and 79:9; Isaiah 17:10; Micah 7:7; 1 Timothy 1:1, 2:3; Titus 1:3, 2:10, and 3:4; Jude 1:25)

God the (our) Father (Romans 1:7; Galatians 1:1–4; Ephesians 5:20; Colossians 3:17; 2 Thessalonians 2:16–17; James 1:27; 2 Peter 1:17; 2 John 1:3; Revelation 1:6)

God the Father of our Lord Christ Jesus (Romans 15:6; 2 Corinthians 1:3, 11:31; Ephesians 1:3, 1:17; Colossians 1:3; 1 Peter 1:3)

God who avenges me (Psalms 18:47–48, 94:1; Jeremiah 51:36; Nahum 1:2–3; Romans 12:17–21)

God who forgets sins (Isaiah 38:17, 43:25; Jeremiah 31:34; Micah 7:19; Hebrews 8:12, 10:17)

God who forgives sins (Exodus 34:6–7; Nehemiah 9:17; Psalms 99:8, 130:3–4; Matthew 6:12; Luke 23:34; Acts 2:38; Ephesians 1:7; Colossians 2:13; 1 John 1:9)

God who gives life to the dead (1 Kings 17:17–24; 2 Kings 4:18–37; Mark 5:35–43; Luke 7:12–16; John 5:21, 11:1–45; Romans 4:17; Hebrews 11:17–19, 13:20)

God who rides on the clouds (Deuteronomy 33:26; Psalms 68:4, 104:3; Isaiah 19:1; Daniel 7:13; Matthew 26:64; Luke 21:27; Acts 1:9–11; Revelation 1:7)

God who works wonders (Exodus 15:11; 1 Chronicles 16:8–12; Job 37:14–42:6; Psalms 40:5, 77:14–15, 107, and 136; Luke 13:17; Acts 2:22; Hebrews 2:4)

God, compassionate (Exodus 22:27, 34:6; 2 Chronicles 30:9; Nehemiah 9:17; Psalms 86:15, 103:8, 111:4, and 145:8; Lamentations 3:22; Joel 2:13)

God, eternal (Genesis 21:33; Deuteronomy 32:40, 33:27; Psalms 48:14, 102:25–27; Isaiah 40:28; Daniel 4:34, 6:26; Romans 16:26; Hebrews 1:12; Revelation 4:9, 10:6, and 15:7)

God, gracious (Genesis 21:1; Exodus 34:6; 2 Kings 13:23; 2 Chronicles 30:9; Ezra 9:8; Nehemiah 9:17, 9:31; Psalms 86:15, 103:8, and 111:4; Isaiah 30:18–19; Joel 2:13)

God, great, mighty, awesome (Deuteronomy 7:21, 10:17; Nehemiah 1:5, 4:14, and 9:32; Jeremiah 32:18; Daniel 9:4)

God, immortal (Romans 1:23)

God, living (Deuteronomy 5:26; Joshua 3:10; 1 Samuel 17:26; 2 Kings 19:4; Daniel 6:20; Matthew 16:16; 2 Corinthians 3:3; 1 Timothy 3:15; Hebrew 9:14; Revelation 7:2)

God, merciful (Genesis 19:16; Deuteronomy 4:31; 1 Chronicles 21:13; Nehemiah 9:31; Psalm 78:38; Isaiah 63:9; Daniel 9:9; Luke 1:50; Ephesians 2:4; 1 Peter 1:3)

God, my (Genesis 28:21; Psalms 22:1, 22:10, and 40:5; John 20:17, 20:28; Revelation 3:12)

God, one and only true (Isaiah 45:5; Jeremiah 10:10; John 5:44; 17:3; 1 Timothy 1:17; 1 John 5:20; Revelation 3:7)

God, our (your) (Exodus 6:7; Leviticus 11:45, 26:12; Deuteronomy 32:3; 1 Samuel 2:2; 2 Samuel 22:32; Psalm 77:13; Isaiah 62:5; Revelation 19:1, 19:5)

God, righteous (Psalms 4:1, 7:9; Daniel 9:14)

Good (1 Chronicles 16:34; 2 Chronicles 5:13; Psalms 25:7–8, 34:8, 106:1, 107:1, and 118:1; Jeremiah 33:11; Nahum 1:7; Matthew 19:17; Mark 10:18; 1 Peter 2:2–3)

Good news of peace (Acts 10:36)

Goodness (Exodus 33:19; 2 Chronicles 6:41; Psalms 23:6, 116:12; Hebrews 6:5; 2 Peter 1:3)

Goodness of your love (Psalms 69:16, 109:21)

Goodness, great (abundant) (Nehemiah 9:25, 9:35; Psalms 31:19, 145:7)

Gospel, eternal (Revelation 14:6)

Grace (Proverbs 3:34; John 1:16–17; Acts 18:27; Romans 4:16, 5:2–21, 6:14–15, and 11:5–6; 2 Corinthians 12:9; Ephesians 2:5–10)

Grace and peace (Romans 1:7; 1 Corinthians 1:3; 2 Corinthians 1:2; Galatians 1:3; Ephesians 1:2, 6:23–24; Philippians 1:2; Colossians 1:2; 1 Thessalonians 1:1; Titus 1:4; Revelation 1:4)

Grace of God (the Lord) (Luke 2:40; Acts 11:23, 13:43, 14:26, and 15:40; 1 Corinthians 15:10; 2 Corinthians 1:12; Galatians 1:15, 2:21, and 3:18; Titus 2:11; Hebrews 2:9, 12:15)

Grace of our Lord Jesus Christ (Acts 15:11; Romans 16:20; 1 Corinthians 16:23; 2 Corinthians 8:9, 13:14; Galatians 1:6, 6:18; Philippians 4:23; 1 Thessalonians 5:28; Revelation 22:21)

Grace, gift of (given) (Romans 12:3, 12:6, and 15:15; 1 Corinthians 1:4, 3:10; Galatians 2:9; Ephesians 3:7, 4:7; 2 Timothy 1:9)

Grace, glorious, freely given (Ephesians 1:6–7)

Grace, gospel (message) of God's (Acts 14:3, 20:24; 1 Peter 1:10)

Grace, incomparable riches of (Ephesians 1:7; 2:7)

Grace, mercy, and peace (1 Timothy 1:2; 2 Timothy 1:2; 2 John 1:3)

Grace, saving (Ephesians 2:5, 2:8; Titus 2:11)

Grace, surpassing (full) (John 1:14; Acts 4:33, 6:8; Romans 5:15–17, 5:20, and 8:32;

2 Corinthians 9:8, 9:14; 1 Timothy 1:14; James 4:6; 1 Peter 1:2)

Grace, word of His (Acts 20:32)

Great (Deuteronomy 7:21, 10:17; 2 Samuel 7:22; Nehemiah 1:5, 4:14, 8:6, and 9:32; Job 36:26; Psalms 48:1, 86:10, 95:3, 99:2, and 104:1; Jeremiah 10:6, 32:18; Malachi 1:5; Titus 2:13)

Greater (Exodus 18:11; 2 Chronicles 2:5; Psalm 135:5; Matthew 12:6, 41–42; John 3:30, 10:29; 1 John 3:20, 4:4)

Guest (Genesis 18; Matthew 9:10–11, 26:6–7, and 26:17–19; Mark 2:15, 14:3; Luke 5:29, 7:36, 10:38, 14:1, 19:7, 22:10–12, and 24:29; John 12:1–3; Revelation 3:20)

Guide (Exodus 15:13; Psalms 23:3, 48:14, and 139:9–10; Isaiah 42:16, 58:11; John 16:13)

H

Hand(s), gracious (Exodus 33:21–23; Ezra 7:9, 8:21–23; Nehemiah 2:8, 2:18; Psalm 37:23–24; Isaiah 64:8; Jeremiah 1:9; Mark 7:32–35; Luke 23:46; John 20:20, 20:27)

Hand, mighty (Exodus 6:1, 13:14; Deuteronomy 4:34; Nehemiah 1:10; 1 Peter 5:6)

Hand, right (Exodus 15:6; Psalms 16:11, 18:35, 118:15–16, and 139:9–10; Revelation 1:16, 5:1, 5:7)

Hands, palms of (Isaiah 49:16)

He cares for you (watches over) (Deuteronomy 32:10–11; Psalms 1:6, 27:10, and 131; Hosea 11:1–4; Nahum 1:7; Zephaniah 2:7; Zechariah 10:3; 1 Peter 5:7)

Head (Colossians 2:19)

Head over every power and authority (Colossians 2:10)

Head of every man (1 Corinthians 11:3)

Head of the body (Colossians 1:18)

Head of the church (Ephesians 1:22, 5:23)

Healer (Exodus 15:26; Deuteronomy 32:39; Psalm 147:3; Isaiah 53:5, 57:18–19; Matthew 11:4–5; Acts 9:34–35)

Heir (Psalm 2:8; Matthew 21:38; Mark 12:7; Luke 20:14; Romans 8:17)

Heir of all things (Hebrews 1:2)

Helmet of salvation (Isaiah 59:16–17; Ephesians 6:17; 1 Thessalonians 5:8)

Help (Genesis 4:1; Exodus 2:23–25; 2 Chronicles 14:11; Psalms 30:10, 33:20, 40:17, 46:1, 54:4, 63:7, 115:9–11, and 124:8; Daniel 6:11; Matthew 15:25; Mark 9:24; Hebrews 4:16)

Helper (Exodus 18:4; Deuteronomy 33:29; 2 Samuel 22:30; Psalms 10:14, 27:9, and 118:7; Isaiah 41:13–14, 50:7–9; Romans 8:26; 2 Timothy 1:14; Hebrews 2:18, 13:6)

Hiding place (Psalms 17:8, 27:5, 31:20, 32:7, and 143:9; Isaiah 4:5–6)

High and exalted one (Exodus 15:1; Isaiah 52:13, 57:15; Acts 5:31; Philippians 2:9)

Holiness (1 Corinthians 1:30)

Holy and Righteous One (Acts 3:14)

Holy One (Leviticus 11:44, 19:2; Psalms 16:10, 22:3; Isaiah 43:15; Hosea 11:9; Habakkuk 1:12; Luke 1:35; Acts 2:27, 13:35; 1 John 2:20; Revelation 3:7, 16:5)

Holy One of God (Mark 1:24; Luke 4:34; John 6:68–69)

Holy One of Israel (2 Kings 19:22; Psalms 71:22, 78:41, and 89:18; Isaiah 1:4, 10:20, 12:6, 30:11–15, 41:14–16, 43:3, 54:5, and 55:5; Ezekiel 39:7)

Holy One of Jacob (Isaiah 29:23)

Holy, holy, holy (Isaiah 6:1–3; Revelation 4:8)

Honey (Exodus 3:8, 16:31; Leviticus 20:24; Psalms 19:9–10, 81:16, and 119:103)

Hope (Psalms 65:5, 71:5, and 119:49; Jeremiah 29:11; Romans 5:5; 2 Corinthians 3:12; Ephesians 1:18, 4:4; Colossians 1:3–6; 1 Timothy 1:1; Titus 2:13; Hebrews 6:18–19, 10:23)

Hope of eternal life (Titus 1:2, 3:7)

Hope of glory (Luke 2:8–11; Romans 5:2; Colossians 1:27)

Hope of Israel (Jeremiah 14:8, 17:13; Acts 28:20)

Hope of salvation (Romans 8:24–25; 1 Thessalonians 5:8)

Hope of their fathers (Jeremiah 50:7)

Hope, better (Hebrews 7:19)

Hope, living (1 Peter 1:3)

Horn of (my) salvation (Exodus 27:2; 2 Samuel 22:3; Psalm 18:2; Luke 1:69)

Horn of David (Israel) (Psalm 132:17; Ezekiel 29:21)

House for the Name of the Lord (Exodus 15:13; Deuteronomy 12:5, 12:11, and 16:2; 2 Samuel 7:13; 1 Chronicles 22:8; 2 Chronicles 7:16; Jeremiah 7:11)

House of prayer (Isaiah 56:7; Matthew 21:13; Mark 11:17; Luke 19:46)

House of the Lord (God) (1 Samuel 1:7, 1:24; 1 Chronicles 6:48, 9:23, and 22:11; Psalms 23:6, 27:4, and 84:4; Hebrews 3:5–6, 10:21)

House, my Father's (Psalm 69:9; Luke 2:49; John 2:16, 14:2)

Husband (Isaiah 54:5; Jeremiah 3:14, 3:20, and 31:32; Hosea 2:16; 2 Corinthians 11:2; Ephesians 5:23–32; Revelation 21:2)

I

I AM (JAH, JEHOVAH) (Exodus 3:14; John 8:58, 18:5–8)

I AM COMING SOON (Matthew 24:27; Luke 21:27; Hebrews 10:37; James 5:8; Revelation 1:7, 3:11, 22:7, 22:12, and 22:20)

Image of the invisible God (2 Corinthians 4:4; Colossians 1:15; Hebrews 1:3)

Immanuel (Psalm 23:4; Isaiah 7:14, 43:2, and 43:5; Matthew 1:23, 28:20)

Inheritance (Numbers 18:20; Deuteronomy 10:9, 18:2; Joshua 13:33; Psalms 16:5, 119:111; Ezekiel 44:28; Acts 20:32; Ephesians 1:14, 1:18; Colossians 3:24)

Inheritance (Portion) of Jacob (Jeremiah 51:19)

Inheritance, eternal (Hebrews 9:15; 1 Peter 1:4)

Intercessor (Isaiah 53:12; Romans 8:26–27, 8:34; Hebrews 7:25, 9:24)

J

Jasper (Revelation 4:3)

Jealous (Exodus 20:5, 34:14; Deuteronomy 4:24, 5:9, and 6:15; Joshua 24:19; Nahum 1:2; 1 Corinthians 10:22)

Jehovah-jireh (Genesis 22:14; Philippians 4:19)

Jerusalem, heavenly (new, above) (Zechariah 8:3; Galatians 4:26; Hebrews 12:22; Revelation 3:12, 21:2, and 21:10)

Jesus (Matthew 1:16, 1:21, 1:25, 27:37, and 28:18; Mark 1:9, 15:37; Luke 2:21, 2:52, and 24:36; John 1:36, 21:25; Acts 1:11; Philippians 2:9–11; Hebrews 12:2; Revelation 22:16)

Jesus Christ (Matthew 1:1, 1:18; Mark 1:1; John 1:17, 17:3; Acts 2:38; Romans 1:6; 1 Corinthians 3:11; Hebrews 13:8; 1 Peter 1:13; 1 John 3:16; Revelation 1:2, 1:5)

Jesus (Christ) crucified (Matthew 27:32–54; Mark 15:24–32; Luke 23:26–43; John 19:16–24; Acts 2:36; 1 Corinthians 1:23, 2:2; Galatians 3:1, 6:14; Hebrews 12:2; Revelation 11:8)

Jesus (Christ) hung on a tree (Acts 5:30, 10:39, and 13:29; 1 Peter 2:24)

Jesus Christ our Savior (Titus 3:6)

Jesus Christ resurrected (Psalm 16:10; Matthew 16:21, 28:1–10; Luke 24:1–12; John 20; Acts 2:23–24; Romans 10:9; 1 Corinthians 15:4; Ephesians 1:20; 1 Peter 1:3)

Jesus Christ same yesterday, today and forever (Hebrews 13:8)

Jesus Christ under God's curse (Deuteronomy 21:22–23; Galatians 3:13)

Jesus lives forever (Hebrews 7:24)

Jesus of Galilee (Matthew 21:11, 26:69)

Jesus of Nazareth (Matthew 21:11, 26:71; Mark 1:24, 10:47; Luke 4:34, 24:19; John 1:45; Acts 2:22, 10:38, and 22:8)

Joy (of the Lord, Spirit) (Nehemiah 8:10; Psalm 16:11; John 17:13; Acts 2:25–28, 13:52; Romans 14:17, 15:13; Galatians 5:22; 1 Peter 1:8; 4:13; Jude 1:24)

Joy, everlasting (Isaiah 35:10, 51:11, and 61:7)

Judge (Deuteronomy 32:36; Judges 11:27; Psalms 50:6, 75:7; Isaiah 11:4, 16:5, and

33:22; 1 Corinthians 4:4; James 4:12, 5:9;
1 Peter 4:5)

Judge of all the earth (of all men) (Genesis 18:25; Psalm 94:2; Hebrews 12:23)

Judge of the living and the dead (Acts 10:42; 2 Timothy 4:1; Revelation 20:12–13)

Judge, righteous (Psalms 7:11, 9:8; 2 Timothy 4:8)

Just One (KJV) (Matthew 27:19, 27:24; Acts 3:14, 7:52, and 22:14; 1 Peter 3:18)

K

Keeper (Numbers 6:24; Psalms 17:8, 27:5, and 121:7; 1 Corinthians 1:8; Jude 1:24)

Keeper of the covenant of love (Deuteronomy 4:31, 7:9, and 7:12; 1 Kings 8:23; Nehemiah 1:5, 9:32; Psalm 89:28; Isaiah 54:10; Daniel 9:4; 2 Peter 3:8–9)

Kind (kindness) (Isaiah 63:7; Jeremiah 9:24; Hosea 11:4; Romans 2:4, 11:22; Ephesians 2:7; Titus 3:4)

Kindness and love of God (Titus 3:4)

Kindness, everlasting (unfailing) (2 Samuel 22:51; Psalm 18:50; Isaiah 54:8)

King (Psalms 2:6, 29:10, 45:1, 99:4, and 145:1; Isaiah 6:5; Jeremiah 23:5; Zechariah 14:16; John 18:37; Acts 17:7)

King of glory (Psalm 24:7–10)

King of heaven (heaven rules) (Daniel 4:26, 4:37)

King of Israel (Isaiah 44:6; Zephaniah 3:15; Matthew 27:42; Mark 15:32; John 1:49, 12:13)

King of Jacob (Isaiah 41:21)

King of Kings (1 Timothy 6:15; Revelation 17:14, 19:16)

King of peace (Salem) (Genesis 14:18; Hebrews 7:1–2)

King of righteousness (Zechariah 9:9; Hebrews 7:2)

King of the ages (Revelation 15:3)

King of the Jews (Matthew 2:2, 27:37; Mark 15:9–26; Luke 23:37–38; John 18:33–39, 19:19–22)

King of the nations (Psalm 22:28; Jeremiah 10:7)

King over all the earth (Psalm 47:2, 47:7; Zechariah 14:9)

King, eternal (Psalms 10:16, 29:10; Jeremiah 10:10; 1 Timothy 1:17)

King, gentle (Zechariah 9:9; Matthew 21:5)

King, great (Psalms 48:2, 95:3; Malachi 1:14; Matthew 5:35)

King, immortal (1 Timothy 1:17; 6:16)

King, invisible (1 Timothy 1:17, 6:15–16)

King, my (our) (your) (1 Samuel 12:12; Psalms 5:2, 44:4, and 84:3; Isaiah 33:22, 43:15; Zechariah 9:9; Matthew 21:5; John 12:15, 19:14–15)

Kingdom (1 Chronicles 29:11; Psalms 45:6, 103:19, and 145:11–13; Obadiah 1:21; Matthew 6:10, 6:33, and 16:28; 1 Thessalonians 2:12)

Kingdom of Christ (Luke 22:29–30; John 18:36; 1 Corinthians 15:22–24; Ephesians 5:5; Colossians 1:13; Revelation 11:15)

Kingdom of God (heaven) (Matthew 3:2, 5:3, 5:10, and 18:1–4; Mark 1:15, 10:14–15, 12:34, and 14:24; Luke 10:9–11, 17:20–21, and 23:51; John 3:3–5; Acts 1:3, 28:30; 2 Timothy 4:18; Revelation 12:10)

Kingdom of good news (Matthew 4:23; Luke 8:1; Acts 8:12)

Kingdom of light (Colossians 1:12–13)

Kingdom of my Father (Matthew 26:29)

Kingdom of Son whom he loves (Colossians 1:12)

Kingdom, eternal (Psalm 145:13; Daniel 2:44, 4:3, 4:34, and 7:27; Luke 1:33; Hebrews 12:28; 2 Peter 1:11)

Kinsman-redeemer (Ruth 4:14)

L

Lamb (Genesis 22:8; Exodus 12:21; Revelation 5:8, 5:13, 6:1, 6:16, 7:9–10, 7:14, 14:4, 14:10, 15:3, 17:14, 19:7–9, 21:14, 21:22–23, 21:27, 22:1, and 22:3)

Lamb (He) who overcomes (John 16:33; Revelation 3:21, 17:14)

Lamb in center of throne (Revelation 7:17)

Lamb of God who takes away the sins of the world (John 1:29)

Lamb slain (Genesis 22:13–14; Exodus 12:21; Isaiah 53:7; Mark 14:12; Luke 22:7; 1 Corinthians 5:7; Revelation 5:6, 5:12, and 13:8)

Lamb standing on Mount Zion (Revelation 14:1)

Lamb without spot or blemish (Exodus 12:5; Hebrews 9:14; 1 Peter 1:18–19)

Lamp (Exodus 25:31–37; Leviticus 24:2–4; 2 Samuel 22:29; Psalms 18:28, 119:105; Proverbs 20:27; Zechariah 4:1–6; Revelation 1:12–13, 21:23)

Lawgiver (Isaiah 33:22; James 4:12)

Leader and commander of the peoples (Isaiah 55:4)

Life (John 1:4, 5:26, 11:25, and 14:6; 1 Timothy 6:19; 1 John 1:2, 5:11–12)

Life, eternal (John 10:28, 17:1–3; 1 John 1:2, 5:11, and 5:20)

Life, new (Acts 5:20; Romans 6:4)

Life, our (your) (Deuteronomy 30:20; Galatians 2:20; Philippians 1:21; Colossians 3:3–4)

Lifter of my head (Psalms 3:3, 27:6)

Light (Genesis 1:3–5; Psalms 27:1, 36:9; Micah 7:8; John 1:5, 3:19–21, and 12:35–36; Acts 9:3, 26:13, and 26:23; 2 Corinthians 4:6; Ephesians 5:13–14; 1 John 1:5–7)

Light of Israel (Isaiah 10:17)

Light of life (John 1:4, 8:12)

Light of the world (of men) (John 1:4, 8:12, 9:5, and 12:46)

Light to the Gentiles (Isaiah 42:6, 49:6; Luke 2:32; Acts 13:47–48)

Light, everlasting (Isaiah 60:19–20; Revelation 22:5)

Light, great (Isaiah 9:2; Matthew 4:16)

Light, true (John 1:9; 1 John 2:8)

Light, unapproachable (1 Timothy 6:14–16)

Light, wonderful (1 Peter 2:9)

Lily of the valleys (Song of Songs 2:1)

Lion of the tribe of Judah (Genesis 49:8–10; Isaiah 31:4; Jeremiah 25:38; Hosea 11:9–11; Joel 3:16; Amos 3:6–8; Matthew 27:50–54; Revelation 5:4–5)

Living One (Luke 24:5; Revelation 1:18)

LORD (Jehovah/Yahweh, indicated in the NIV by LORD and mentioned over seven thousand times in the Old Testament: self-existing one)

Lord Almighty (1 Samuel 1:3, 1:11; Psalms 24:10, 46:7, and 46:11; Isaiah 54:5; Zechariah 8; Malachi; Romans 9:29; 2 Corinthians 6:18; James 5:4)

Lord and Savior Jesus Christ (2 Peter 1:11, 2:20, and 3:18)

Lord between the cherubim (Ark, mercy seat) (Exodus 25:17–22; Numbers 7:89; 1 Samuel 4:4; 2 Samuel 6:2; 2 Kings 19:15; 1 Chronicles 13:6; Psalm 80:1; Isaiah 37:16)

Lord of both the dead and the living (Romans 14:9)

Lord God (Genesis 2; 3; Revelation 18:8)

Lord God Almighty (2 Samuel 5:10; 1 Kings 19:10; Psalm 89:8; Amos 4:13; Revelation 4:8, 19:6, and 21:22)

Lord Jesus (Mark 16:19; Luke 24:3; Acts 4:33; 1 Corinthians 11:23; Revelation 22:20–21)

Lord Jesus Christ (Acts 11:17, 28:31; Romans 13:14; Ephesians 1:2; Colossians 2:6; 1 Thessalonians 5:9, 5:23, and 5:28; Philemon 1:3, 1:25; 1 Peter 1:3; 2 Peter 1:8, 1:14, and 1:16; Jude 1:21)

Lord mighty in battle (1 Samuel 17:47; 1 Chronicles 5:22; 2 Chronicles 20:15; Psalm 24:8)

Lord Most High (Psalms 7:17, 47:2)

Lord of all (Acts 10:36; Romans 10:12)

Lord of all the earth (Joshua 3:11–13; Psalm 24:1; Micah 4:13; Zechariah 6:5)

Lord of glory (Exodus 16:7, 16:10, and 40:34–35; Deuteronomy 5:24; Psalm 138:5; Isaiah

60:1; Ezekiel 43:2–5; Habakkuk 2:14; 1 Corinthians 2:8)

Lord of heaven and earth (Matthew 11:25; Acts 17:24)

Lord of kings (Daniel 2:47)

Lord of lords (Deuteronomy 10:17; Psalm 136:3; 1 Timothy 6:15; Revelation 17:14, 19:16)

Lord of peace (2 Thessalonians 3:16)

Lord of Sabbath (Matthew 12:8; Mark 2:28; Luke 6:5)

Lord of the harvest (Matthew 9:38; Luke 10:2)

Lord our (your) God (Exodus 3:18, 20:2–7; Leviticus 11:44; Deuteronomy 4:7, 6:1–5, 31:6; 1 Kings 8:57–61; Isaiah 43:3; Joel 2:26–27; Acts 2:38–39; Revelation 4:11)

Lord, our righteousness (Jeremiah 23:6, 33:16; 1 Corinthians 1:30)

Lord who blesses (Genesis 1:22, 1:28, and 12:2–3; Deuteronomy 11:26–28, 28:1–14; Zechariah 4:7; Matthew 5:3–11, 21:9; Luke 24:51; John 1:16; Ephesians 1:3)

Lord who brings you out (Genesis 15:7; Exodus 13:3, 16:6; Leviticus 11:45; Numbers 15:41; Deuteronomy 5:6; Joshua 24:17; Judges 2:12; 1 Kings 9:9)

Lord who carries you like a father carries a son (Deuteronomy 1:31; Isaiah 46:3–4, 63:9)

Lord who carries you on eagle's wings (Exodus 19:4; Deuteronomy 32:11)

Lord who delights in me (Deuteronomy 30:9; 2 Samuel 22:20; Psalms 147:11, 149:4; Proverbs 12:22; Isaiah 62:4, 65:19; Zephaniah 3:17)

Lord who disciplines you like a man disciplines his son (Deuteronomy 8:5; Hebrews 12:5–9)

Lord who dwells (Exodus 25:8, 29:45–46; Numbers 35:34; Ezekiel 37:27–28; Zechariah 8:3; Matthew 18:20; John 1:14; Ephesians 3:17; Revelation 21:3)

Lord who goes before you (Deuteronomy 1:30–33, 9:3, and 31:8; Isaiah 45:2, 52:12; Micah 2:13)

Lord who goes behind you (Exodus 14:19–20; Isaiah 52:12, 58:8)

Lord who goes with you (Deuteronomy 20:4, 31:6)

Lord who hears (Genesis 16:11, 21:17; Exodus 2:24; Numbers 11:1; 2 Chronicles 7:14; Psalms 6:8–9, 116:1–2; Jonah 2:2; John 11:41–42; Acts 10:31; 1 Peter 3:12)

Lord who is with me (Genesis 3:8, 12:7, and 28:15; Exodus 33:14–17; Deuteronomy 4:7; Joshua 1:5; Psalm 139:7; Jeremiah 1:8; Matthew 28:20; John 14:3; Acts 18:10; Revelation 21:3)

Lord who knows (1 Samuel 2:3; Psalms 94:11, 139:1–4, and 139:23; Matthew 6:8, 9:4; Luke 9:47; John 10:14; Acts 1:24, 15:8; Romans 8:27; 1 Corinthians 8:3, 13:12; 1 John 3:20)

Lord who redeems you (Exodus 6:6; 2 Samuel 7:23; 1 Chronicles 17:21; Psalm 44:26; Hosea 13:14; Zechariah 10:8; Galatians 3:13–14, 4:5; Titus 2:14; 1 Peter 1:18–19)

Lord who reigns (Exodus 15:18; 1 Chronicles 16:31; Psalm 97:1; Lamentations 5:19; Luke 1:32–33; 1 Corinthians 15:25; Revelation 11:15–17, 19:6)

Lord who rescues (Exodus 3:8; 2 Samuel 22:18–20; Isaiah 46:4; Jeremiah 1:8, 20:13; Daniel 6:27; Luke 1:74; Galatians 1:4; Colossians 1:13; 1 Thessalonians 1:10)

Lord who sanctifies you (makes holy) (Exodus 31:13; Leviticus 20:8; John 17:17–19; 1 Thessalonians 5:23; Hebrews 2:11)

Lord who saves (2 Chronicles 20:9; Isaiah 33:22; Ezekiel 34:22; Daniel 3:17, 3:29; Zephaniah 3:17; Matthew 1:21; John 3:16–17; 1 Timothy 1:15; Hebrews 7:25)

Lord who searches (Genesis 3:9; Psalms 7:9, 139:1, and 139:23; Jeremiah 17:10; Ezekiel 34:11, 34:16; Luke 15, 19:10; Romans 8:27; 1 Corinthians 2:10; Revelation 2:23)

Lord who sees (Genesis 6:5, 16:13; Exodus 3:7; 2 Chronicles 16:9; Job 34:21; Psalms

33:13–14, 94:9; Proverbs 15:3; Zechariah 4:10; 1 Peter 3:12)

Lord who sits on throne (1 Kings 22:19; Psalm 47:8; Isaiah 6:1; Matthew 25:31; Revelation 4:2, 4:9–10, 5:1, 5:7, 5:13, 7:15, and 21:5)

Lord who walks with (Genesis 3:8, 5:24; Leviticus 26:12; Daniel 3:25; Micah 6:8; Malachi 2:6; Mark 1:16–19; Luke 24:15; 2 Corinthians 6:16; Revelation 3:4)

Love (Psalm 144:2; Isaiah 63:9; Zephaniah 3:17; John 3:16, 13:1, and 13:34; Romans 5:5, 5:8, and 8:35–39; 2 Corinthians 13:14; Titus 3:4; 1 John 4:8–16)

Love, abounding (Exodus 34:6; Nehemiah 9:17; Psalms 86:5, 86:15, and 103:8; Joel 2:13; Jonah 4:2; Ephesians 3:17–19)

Love, eternal (enduring) (1 Kings 10:9; 1 Chronicles 16:34; 2 Chronicles 20:21; Ezra 3:11; Psalms 100:5, 118:1–4, and 118:136; Jeremiah 31:3, 33:11)

Love, first (Revelation 2:4)

Love, great (Numbers 14:19; Psalms 57:10, 69:13, 86:13, 103:11, 106:45, 108:4, and 117; Lamentations 3:22; John 15:13; Ephesians 2:4; 1 John 3:1)

Love, unfailing (Exodus 15:13; Psalms 6:4, 13:5, 33:5, 33:18, 44:26, 51:1–2, 119:76, and 147:11; Isaiah 54:10; Lamentations 3:32)

M

Majesty (exaltation) (Exodus 15:7; Deuteronomy 33:26; 1 Chronicles 16:27; Psalms 8:1, 8:9, 93:1, and 145:5; Isaiah 2:10, 2:19, and 2:21; 2 Peter 1:16–17; Jude 25)

Majesty in heaven (Hebrews 1:3, 8:1)

Maker (Job 4:17, 32:22, and 36:3; Psalms 95:6, 121:2, and 149:2; Proverbs 22:2; Ecclesiastes 11:5; Isaiah 45:9, 54:5; Jeremiah 51:19; Hosea 8:14)

Man approved of God (Acts 2:22)

Man Christ Jesus (Romans 5:15; 1 Timothy 2:5)

Man of sorrows (Isaiah 53:3; John 19:1–5)

Man, appointed (Acts 17:31)

Man, fourth in the fiery furnace (Daniel 3:25)

Man, second (1 Corinthians 15:47)

Master (Malachi 1:6; Matthew 23:8, 24:45–50, and 25:19–30; Luke 5:5, 8:24, 8:45, 9:33, 9:49, and 17:13; John 13:16, 15:20; Ephesians 6:9; Colossians 4:1; 2 Timothy 2:21)

Mediator between God and man (1 Timothy 2:5)

Mediator of new covenant (Hebrews 8:6, 9:15, and 12:24)

Mediator, one (1 Timothy 2:5)

Mercy (Exodus 33:19; Deuteronomy 13:17; Psalms 40:11, 57:1, and 123; Micah 7:18; Zechariah 1:16; Romans 9:15, 11:30–32, and 15:9; Titus 3:5; Hebrews 4:16; James 5:11; 1 Peter 2:10)

Mercy seat (KJV) (Exodus 25:17–22, 30:6; Leviticus 16:2; Numbers 7:89)

Mercy, great (rich) (2 Samuel 24:14; 1 Chronicles 21:13; Nehemiah 9:31; Psalms 5:7, 25:6, and 69:16; Daniel 9:18; Luke 1:58; Ephesians 2:4; 1 Peter 1:3)

Messenger of the (new) covenant (Malachi 3:1)

Messiah (anointed one) (Daniel 9:25–26; John 1:40–42, 4:25–26)

Mighty God (Deuteronomy 10:17; Isaiah 9:6, 10:21; Luke 22:69)

Mighty One (Joshua 22:22; Job 34:17; Psalm 50:1; Isaiah 10:34; Matthew 26:64; Luke 1:49)

Mighty One of Jacob (Israel) (Genesis 49:24; Psalms 132:2, 132:5; Isaiah 1:24, 49:26, and 60:16)

Mighty to save (Isaiah 63:1; Zephaniah 3:17)

Milk, pure spiritual (Exodus 3:8; Isaiah 55:1; 1 Peter 2:2)

Most High (Deuteronomy 32:8; 2 Samuel 22:14; Psalms 21:7, 82:6, 91:1, 91:9–10, and 97:9; Luke 1:32, 1:35, and 6:35)

Most Holy Place (Holy of Holies) (Exodus 26:33–34; Leviticus 16; 1 Kings 8:6; Psalm 28:2; Hebrews 9:3–12, 10:19–20, and 13:11–13)

Myrrh, bundle of (Song of Solomon 1:13)

Mystery of Christ (Ephesians 3:4; Colossians 4:3)

Mystery of God (Colossians 2:2–3; Revelation 10:7)

Mystery of His will (Ephesians 1:7–10)

Mystery, hidden (Romans 16:25–26; Ephesians 3:9; Colossians 1:26)

Mystery, profound (Ephesians 5:32)

N

Nail (peg) in a sure (firm) place (Ezra 9:8, KJV; Isaiah 22:23; Zechariah 10:4; John 20:25, 20:27)

Name on forehead (Revelation 3:12, 14:1, and 22:4)

Nazarene, the (Jesus of Nazareth) (Matthew 2:23; Mark 1:24, 14:67, and 16:6; John 18:5, 18:7, and 19:19; Acts 2:22, 3:6, 4:10, and 6:14)

O

Offering and sacrifice to God (Ephesians 5:2; Hebrews 9:26, 10:10–14)

Offering, burnt (Genesis 8:20, 22:2–13; Leviticus 1:3–17; Micah 6:6–8; Mark 12:33; Hebrews 10:5–10)

Offering, drink (Exodus 29:40–41; Numbers 28:7–10, 29:18–39; Matthew 20:22–23; John 6:55; 18:11)

Offering, grain (Exodus 29:41; Leviticus 2:1–16; John 6)

Offering, guilt (Leviticus 5:15–19, 7:1–7; Isaiah 53:10)

Offering, peace (fellowship) (Leviticus 3; Ephesians 2:13–18)

Offering, sin (Exodus 29:36; Leviticus 4; Romans 8:3; 2 Corinthians 5:21; Hebrews 10:10–14)

Oil (Genesis 28:18; Exodus 27:20, 30:22–33; Psalms 23:5, 45:7, and 133; Isaiah 61:3; Matthew 25:1–13; John 12:1–8; Hebrews 1:9; James 5:14)

One abandoned (Matthew 26:31, 26:56; Mark 14:27, 14:50; John 16:31)

One accused (Matthew 26:60–66, 27:12–14; Luke 23:1–5, 23:10; John 18:30, 19:7)

One anguished (Luke 22:44)

One beaten with fists (Matthew 26:67; Mark 14:65; Luke 22:63)

One betrayed (Matthew 26:20, 47–50; Mark 10:33, 14:18–21, and 43–45; Luke 22:3–6, 22:47–48; John 18:2–3)

One blindfolded (Mark 14:65; Luke 22:64)

One despised (Psalms 22:6, 69:7–10; Isaiah 49:7, 53:3; Mark 9:12; Luke 18:31–33)

One disowned (Matthew 26:34, 69–75; Mark 14:30, 66–72; Luke 22:34, 22:54–62; John 18:17, 18:25–27)

One flogged (Isaiah 50:6, 53:5; Matthew 20:19, 27:26; Mark 10:34; Luke 18:32, 22:63; John 19:1)

One insulted (Psalm 22:7; Matthew 27:39, 27:44; Mark 15:29–32; Luke 18:32, 22:65, 23:35, and 23:39)

One mocked (Psalms 22:7, 69:12, 74:10, 74:18, and 74:22; Matthew 20:19, 27:29, 27:31, and 27:41; Mark 10:34, 15:16–20, and 15:31; Luke 18:32, 22:63, 23:11, and 23:36; John 19:2–3)

One pierced (Luke 24:39–40; John 19:34, 19:37, 20:20, and 20:25–28)

One sent (Isaiah 61:1; Luke 4:18; John 3:34, 5:38, and 6:29; Galatians 4:4; 1 John 4:9)

One slapped in the face (Matthew 26:67; John 18:22, 19:3)

One spat upon (Matthew 26:67, 27:30; Mark 10:34, 14:65, and 15:19; Luke 18:32)

One to be feared (1 Chronicles 16:25; Psalms 76:7–11, 89:7, and 96:4; Malachi 1:14; Matthew 10:28; Luke 12:4–5; Acts 5:5, 5:11, and 19:17)

One who comes (Psalm 118:26; Matthew 3:11, 11:3, and 21:9; Mark 11:9; Luke 7:19–20, 13:35; John 12:13; Revelation 22:20)

One who holds the key of David (Isaiah 22:22; Revelation 3:7)

One who holds the keys of death and Hades (Revelation 1:18, 20:1)

One who is in you (Christ) (2 Corinthians 13:5; Galatians 2:20; Ephesians 3:17; Colossians 1:27; 1 John 4:4)

One who opens (Deuteronomy 28:12; 2 Kings 6:17; Psalm 105:41; Isaiah 22:22; Matthew 7:7–8, 27:52; John 1:51; Acts 5:19; Hebrews 10:20; Revelation 3:7, 20:12)

One who overcomes (triumphed) (Revelation 3:21, 5:5, and 17:14)

One who sends (Matthew 10, 28:16–20; Mark 6:7–12; Luke 9:1–6, 10:1–20; John 20:21; Acts 1:8)

One who shuts (Genesis 7:16; 2 Chronicles 7:13; Isaiah 22:22; Daniel 6:22; Matthew 25:10; Luke 4:25; Revelation 3:7)

Overseer of your souls (1 Peter 2:25)

Owl of the desert (Psalm 102:6)

P

Passover (Exodus 12; 2 Chronicles 35:1–18; 1 Corinthians 5:7; Hebrews 10:1–18)

Pasture, true (Jeremiah 50:7; John 10:9)

Path (way) of peace (Isaiah 59:8; Luke 1:79; Romans 3:17)

Path of life (Psalm 16:11; Proverbs 15:24; Matthew 7:14; Acts 2:28)

Peace (shalom) (Judges 6:24; Psalms 29:11, 85:8, and 85:10; Isaiah 9:7, 26:12; Micah 5:5; Luke 2:14, 24:36; John 14:27, 16:33; John 20:19, 20:21; Romans 5:1; Ephesians 2:14)

Peace like a river (Isaiah 48:18, 66:12)

Peace-giver (Isaiah 26:3; John 14:27, 16:33; Philippians 4:7; Colossians 3:15)

Peace, good news of (Luke 2:14; Acts 10:36; Ephesians 6:15)

Peace, great (Psalm 119:165)

Peace, perfect (Isaiah 26:3)

Pearl of great price (Matthew 13:45–46)

Physician (Isaiah 35:5–6; Matthew 9:12, 11:2–5; Luke 4:16–24)

Pillar of cloud (Exodus 13:21–22, 19:9, 24:15–18, and 33:9–11; Numbers 9:15–23;

Isaiah 4:5–6; Matthew 17:5; Acts 1:9–11; 1 Thessalonians 4:16–18; Revelation 14:14–16)

Pillar of fire (Exodus 13:21–22, 14:24, and 40:38; Numbers 9:15–16, 14:14; Deuteronomy 1:33, 4:11–12, and 4:36; Nehemiah 9:12, 9:19)

Plant of renown (KJV) (Ezekiel 34:29)

Portion of Jacob (Jeremiah 10:16, 51:19)

Portion, my (Psalms 16:5, 73:26, 119:57, and 142:5; Lamentations 3:24)

Possessor of heaven and earth (KJV) (Genesis 14:19, 14:22)

Potter (Isaiah 29:16, 45:9, and 64:8; Jeremiah 18:6; Romans 9:20–21)

Power of God (Exodus 14:31; Psalm 68:34; Isaiah 40:10; Mark 12:24; Romans 4:20–21; 1 Corinthians 1:18, 1:24; Ephesians 1:19–21; Philippians 3:10; Revelation 12:10, 19:1)

Power of our Lord Jesus Christ (Mark 5:30, 13:26; Luke 4:14, 21:27; John 13:3; Acts 10:38; 2 Corinthians 12:9; Philippians 3:10, 3:21; 2 Peter 1:16; Revelation 1:6, 5:12–13)

Power, all surpassing (2 Corinthians 4:7)

Power, eternal (Romans 1:20)

Praise (Deuteronomy 10:21; Psalm 148:14; Jeremiah 17:14)

Priest (Psalm 110:4; Hebrews 7:21, 10:11–12)

Priest on His throne (Zechariah 6:13; Hebrews 8:1, 10:11–13)

Priest, forever in the order of Melchizedek (Genesis 14:18–20; Psalm 110:4; Hebrews 5:6, 5:10, 6:20, and 7:17)

Priest, great high (Hebrews 4:14, 10:21)

Priest, high (Hebrews 2:17, 3:1, 7:26–27, 8:1, and 9:11)

Prince (Ezekiel 34:24; Acts 5:31)

Prince of life (KJ) (Acts 3:15)

Prince of peace (Isaiah 9:6)

Prince of princes (Daniel 8:25)

Promise (Luke 24:49; Acts 1:4, 2:33; Galatians 3:13–14; Ephesians 1:13)

Promise of life (2 Timothy 1:1)

Prophet (Matthew 13:57; Luke 13:33, 24:19)

Prophet from Nazareth in Galilee (Matthew 21:11)

Prophet like Moses (Deuteronomy 18:15, 18:18; Acts 3:22, 7:37)

Prophet who is to come (John 6:14)

Prophet, great (Luke 7:16)

Propitiation (KJV), atonement (Romans 3:25; Hebrews 2:17; 1 John 2:2, 4:10)

Pure (2 Samuel 22:27; Psalm 18:26; Habakkuk 1:13; Hebrews 7:26; 1 John 3:3)

R

Rabbi (teacher or master) (Mark 10:51; John 1:38, 1:49, and 3:2)

Rabboni (my great master) (John 20:16)

Radiance of God's glory (Ezekiel 10:4; John 1:14; Hebrews 1:3)

Rain (Psalm 72:6; Isaiah 45:8; Hosea 6:3)

Rainbow (Genesis 9:8–17; Ezekiel 1:28; Revelation 4:3, 10:1)

Ransom (Psalm 49:7–8; Jeremiah 31:11; Hosea 13:14; Matthew 20:28; Mark 10:45; 1 Timothy 2:6; Hebrews 9:15)

Reconciler (peacemaker) (Romans 5:10–11; 2 Corinthians 5:18–21; Ephesians 2:14–18; Colossians 1:20–23)

Redeemer (Job 19:25; Psalm 19:14; Isaiah 41:14, 43:14, 44:6, 44:24, 54:5, 54:8, 59:20, 60:16, and 63:16; Jeremiah 50:34)

Redemption (Luke 2:38, 21:28; 1 Corinthians 1:30; Ephesians 1:7; Colossians 1:14)

Redemption, eternal (Hebrews 9:12)

Refiner and purifier (Zechariah 13:9; Malachi 3:3)

Refuge (Deuteronomy 33:27; 2 Samuel 22:3; Psalms 9:9, 14:6, 18:2, 46:1, 62:7–8, 71:7, 91:2, 91:9, and 118:8; Proverbs 10:29; Isaiah 57:13; Jeremiah 16:19; Joel 3:16)

Repairer of broken walls (Isaiah 58:12)

Reproach of men (scorned, disgraced) (Psalms 22:6, 31:11, and 69:19–20; Hebrews 13:13)

Rest (Isaiah 30:15; Jeremiah 6:16; Hebrews 4:1–11)

Rest-giver (Genesis 2:2–3; Exodus 33:14; Psalm 62:1, 62:5; Jeremiah 31:2; Matthew 11:28–29)

Restorer (Psalms 23:3, 51:12, 80:3, and 85:4; Isaiah 57:18; Jeremiah 31:18; Lamentations 5:21; Nahum 2:2; Zechariah 10:6; Acts 3:21, 15:16; 1 Peter 5:10)

Restorer of streets with dwellings (Isaiah 58:12)

Resurrection and Life (John 11:25)

Revealer of mysteries (Daniel 2:28–29, 2:47)

Reward (Isaiah 49:4, 62:11; Colossians 3:23–24; Hebrews 11:6; Revelation 22:12)

Reward, great (Genesis 15:1; Matthew 5:12; Luke 6:23, 6:35; Hebrews 10:35)

Reward, sure (Proverbs 11:18; 2 Timothy 4:8)

Riches of His glorious inheritance (Ephesians 1:18)

Riches, glorious (Romans 9:23; Ephesians 3:16; Philippians 4:19; Colossians 1:27)

Riches, unsearchable of Christ (Romans 11:33–36; Ephesians 3:8)

Rider on white horse (Revelation 19:11)

Righteous One (Isaiah 24:16; Acts 3:14, 7:52, and 22:14; 1 Peter 3:18; 1 John 2:1, 2:29, and 3:7)

Righteousness (Psalm 4:1; Jeremiah 23:6, 33:16; 1 Corinthians 1:30)

Righteousness, everlasting (Psalms 111:3, 119:142; Isaiah 51:6, 51:8; Daniel 9:24; Amos 5:24; 2 Corinthians 9:9)

River (Psalms 78:15–16, 105:41; Isaiah 48:21; Ezekiel 47:5; Revelation 22:1)

River of your delights (Psalms 36:8, 46:4)

Rivers, broad, and streams (Isaiah 33:21)

Rock from which you were cut (Isaiah 51:1)

Rock gushing water (Exodus 17:6; Numbers 20:11; Psalms 78:20, 105:41, and 114:8; Isaiah 48:21)

Rock of (my) salvation (Rock, my Savior) (Deuteronomy 32:15; 2 Samuel 22:47; Psalms 89:26, 95:1)

Rock of Israel (Genesis 49:24; 2 Samuel 23:3; Isaiah 30:29)

Rock of my refuge (2 Samuel 22:3; Psalms 18:2, 31:2, 71:3, and 94:22; Isaiah 17:10)

Rock of my strength (KJV) (Psalm 62:7)

Rock of offense (stumbling) (Isaiah 8:14; Romans 9:33; 1 Peter 2:8)

Rock that is higher than I (Psalm 61:2)

Rock who fathered you (Deuteronomy 32:18)

Rock, eternal (Isaiah 26:4)

Rock, huge, in parched land (Isaiah 32:2)

Rock, my (2 Samuel 22:2–3, 22:47; Psalms 18:2, 18:46, 19:14, 28:1, 31:3, 42:9, 62:2, 62:6, 71:3, 92:15, and 144:1)

Rock, spiritual (1 Corinthians 10:4)

Rock, stricken, split (Exodus 17:6; Numbers 20:11; Psalm 78:20; Isaiah 48:21)

Rock, the (our, their) (Deuteronomy 32:4, 32:30–31; 1 Samuel 2:2; 2 Samuel 22:32; Psalms 18:31, 78:35; Isaiah 44:8; Habakkuk 1:12; Matthew 7:24–25; Luke 6:48)

Root of David (Revelation 5:5, 22:16)

Root of Jesse (Isaiah 11:1, 11:10; Romans 15:12)

Root out of a dry ground (Isaiah 53:2)

Rose of Sharon (Song of Solomon 2:1)

Ruler (governor, potentate) (Numbers 24:19; Judges 8:23; 2 Chronicles 20:6; Psalm 22:28; Micah 5:2; Matthew 2:6; 1 Timothy 6:15; Revelation 3:14)

Ruler of the kings of the earth (Revelation 1:5)

Ruler (sovereign) in the kingdom of men (KJV) (Daniel 4:17, 4:25, and 4:32)

S

Sabbath-Rest (Exodus 16:23–29, 20:8–11; Isaiah 58:13; Hebrews 4:1–11)

Sacrifice of atonement (Isaiah 53:10; Romans 3:25; Hebrews 10:12; 1 John 2:2, 4:10)

Salem (Genesis 14:18; Psalm 76:2; Hebrews 7:1–2)

Salvation (my) (Exodus 15:2; Psalms 27:1, 62:2, 62:6, and 118:14; Isaiah 12:2; Luke 2:30; Hebrews 2:3; Revelation 7:10, 12:10, and 19:1)

Salvation, eternal (Isaiah 45:17, 51:6, and 51:8; Hebrews 5:9)

Sanctuary (Exodus 15:17, 25:8; Isaiah 8:14; Ezekiel 11:16)

Savior (Deuteronomy 32:15; 2 Samuel 22:3; Isaiah 43:11; Hosea 13:4; Luke 1:47, 2:11; John 4:42; Acts 5:31; Philippians 3:20; 1 Timothy 4:10; 1 John 4:14)

Savior Jesus Christ (Titus 2:13; 2 Peter 1:1)

Scapegoat in the wilderness (Leviticus 16:21–22; John 19:17; Hebrews 13:12–13)

Scepter from Israel (Numbers 24:17)

Scepter from Judah (Genesis 49:10)

Scepter of justice (Psalm 45:6)

Scepter of righteousness (Hebrews 1:8)

Scepter, iron (Psalm 2:9; Revelation 2:27, 12:5, and 19:15)

Scepter, mighty (Psalm 110:2)

Seal (John 6:27; 2 Corinthians 1:22; Ephesians 1:13, 4:30; 2 Timothy 2:19; Revelation 7:2, 9:4)

Seed (Genesis 3:15; John 12:20–26; Galatians 3:16, 3:19; 1 John 3:9)

Seed of Abraham (Galatians 3:16)

Seed of David (offspring) (Romans 1:3; 2 Timothy 2:8; Revelation 22:16)

Seed, God's (divine) (1 John 3:9)

Seed, imperishable (1 Corinthians 15:50–54; 1 Peter 1:23)

Serpent (bronze) in the wilderness (Numbers 21:9; John 3:14)

Servant (Isaiah 42:1, 49:3, 49:5–7, and 52:13; Zechariah 3:8; Matthew 20:28; Luke 22:27; John 13:1–17; Acts 3:26; Philippians 2:7)

Servant David, my (Ezekiel 34:23–24, 37:24–25; Luke 1:69)

Servant Jesus, holy (glorified) (Acts 3:13, 4:27, and 4:30)

Servant of the Jews (Romans 15:8)

Servant whom I have chosen (Isaiah 42:1; Matthew 12:18)

Servant whom I uphold (Isaiah 42:1)

Servant, righteous (Isaiah 53:11)

Servant, suffering (Isaiah 53)

Shadow (shade) (Psalms 91:1, 121:5; Isaiah 25:4)

Shadow (shelter) of Your wings (Psalms 17:8, 36:7, 57:1, 61:4, 63:7, and 91:4; Isaiah 31:5)

Shadow of His hand (Exodus 33:22; Isaiah 49:2, 51:16)

Shelter (Psalms 27:5, 31:20, and 91:1; Isaiah 4:6, 25:4)

Shepherd (my) (Genesis 49:24; Isaiah 40:11; Jeremiah 31:10; Micah 5:4; Matthew 26:31; Mark 14:27; Revelation 7:17)

Shepherd and guardian of your souls (1 Peter 2:25)

Shepherd of Israel (Psalm 80:1; Matthew 2:6)

Shepherd who carries (Psalm 28:9; Isaiah 40:11, 63:9)

Shepherd who seeks (Ezekiel 34:11–12, 34:16; Luke 15:4–7)

Shepherd who separates (Ezekiel 34:16–22; Matthew 25:31–33)

Shepherd, chief (1 Peter 5:4)

Shepherd, good (John 10:11, 10:14)

Shepherd, great (Hebrews 13:20)

Shepherd, my (Genesis 48:15; Psalm 23:1)

Shepherd, one (Ecclesiastes 12:11; Ezekiel 34:23, 37:24; John 10:16)

Shield (Genesis 15:1; Deuteronomy 33:29; 2 Samuel 22:3, 22:31; Psalms 3:3, 18:2, 18:30, 28:7, 33:20, 84:11, 115:9–11, 119:114, and 144:2; Proverbs 2:7, 30:5; 1 Peter 1:5)

Shield of victory (2 Samuel 22:36; Psalm 18:35)

Shiloh (KJV) (tranquility, rest) (Genesis 49:10)

Shoot, tender (plant) (Isaiah 11:1, 53:2)

Showers (Psalm 72:6; Hosea 10:12)

Soap of launderer (Malachi 3:2)

Son of Abraham (Matthew 1:1; Galatians 3:16)

Son of David (Matthew 1:1, 20:30, and 21:9; Mark 12:35; Luke 1:31–33)

Son of God (Matthew 4:3, 27:40, and 27:54; Mark 1:1, 15:39; Luke 1:35, 22:70; John 1:34, 1:49, and 20:31; Acts 9:20; Romans 1:4; 1 John 5:13)

Son of Joseph (Luke 3:23, 4:22; John 1:45, 6:42)

Son of living God (Matthew 16:16)

Son of Man (Daniel 7:13; Matthew 8:20, 9:6, and 12:8; Mark 2:10, 8:38; Luke 18:8, 21:36, and 24:7; John 1:51, 3:13–14, and 12:34; Revelation 1:13, 14:14)

Son of Man ascended (John 3:13, 6:62, and 20:17; Acts 1:9–11)

Son of Man at the right hand of God (Romans 8:34; 1 Peter 3:21–22)

Son of Man descended (John 3:13)

Son of Man lifted up (John 3:14, 8:28, and 12:32)

Son of Man sitting at the right hand of power (Psalm 110:1; Matthew 26:64; Luke 22:69; Acts 2:33–34; Ephesians 1:20–21; Colossians 3:1; Hebrews 1:3, 12:2; Revelation 3:21)

Son of Man (Lord) standing (at the right hand of God) (Amos 9:1; Zechariah 14:3–4; Acts 7:55–56)

Son of Mary (Matthew 1:25; Mark 6:3; Luke 2:48)

Son of the Blessed One (Mark 14:61)

Son of the Father (2 John 1:3)

Son of the free woman (Galatians 4:30–31)

Son of the Most High God (Mark 5:7; Luke 1:32, 8:28)

Son over God's house (Hebrews 3:6)

Son, beloved (Matthew 3:17, 17:5; Mark 9:7; Luke 3:22; Ephesians 1:6; Colossians 1:13; 2 Peter 1:17)

Son, One and Only (John 1:14, 1:18, 3:16-18; 1 John 4:9)

Song (Exodus 15:1; Psalm 118:14; Isaiah 12:2)

Sovereign LORD (Genesis 15:2; 2 Samuel 7:18–29; Psalm 68:20; Ezekiel (218 references); Habakkuk 3:19; Revelation 6:10)

Sower (Genesis 1:29–30, 2:8–9; Matthew 13:37)

Spirit (Genesis 6:3; Numbers 11:25; Psalm 139:7; Joel 2:28; Zechariah 4:6; Matthew 12:31; John 4:24; Romans 8:26; 2 Corinthians 3:17; Galatians 5:25; Revelation 22:17)

Spirit of adoption (KJV) (Romans 8:15)

Spirit of Christ (Romans 8:9; 1 Peter 1:11)

Spirit of counsel (Isaiah 11:2)

Spirit of fear (awe) of the Lord (Isaiah 11:2)

Spirit of fire (Isaiah 4:4; 1 Thessalonians 5:19)

Spirit of glory (1 Peter 4:14)

Spirit of God (Lord) (Genesis 1:2; Exodus 31:3; 2 Samuel 23:2; Psalm 106:33; Isaiah 11:2, 61:1; Micah 3:8; Matthew 3:16; Acts 8:39; Romans 8:9; Philippians 3:3; 1 John 4:2)

Spirit of grace (Zechariah 12:10; Hebrews 10:29)

Spirit of His Son (Galatians 4:6)

Spirit of holiness (Romans 1:4)

Spirit of Jesus (Acts 16:7)

Spirit of Jesus Christ (Philippians 1:19)

Spirit of judgment (Isaiah 4:4)

Spirit of justice (Isaiah 28:6)

Spirit of knowledge (Isaiah 11:2)

Spirit of life (Romans 8:2, 8:11; 1 Corinthians 15:45; 2 Corinthians 3:6; 1 Peter 3:18)

Spirit of love (Romans 15:30; 2 Timothy 1:7)

Spirit of power (Isaiah 11:2; Romans 15:19; 1 Corinthians 2:4; Galatians 4:29; 2 Timothy 1:7)

Spirit of praise (1 Corinthians 14:15; Ephesians 5:18–19; Colossians 3:16–17)

Spirit of Promise (promised Holy Spirit) (Joel 2:28–29; Luke 24:49; Acts 1:4, 2:16–21, and 2:33; Galatians 3:14; Ephesians 1:13)

Spirit of prophecy (Revelation 19:10)

Spirit of revelation (God reveals) (1 Corinthians 2:9–10; Ephesians 1:17–18)

Spirit of self-discipline (2 Timothy 1:7)

Spirit of sonship (Romans 8:15)

Spirit of supplication (intercedes) (Zechariah 12:10; Romans 8:26)

Spirit of Truth (John 14:17, 15:26, and 16:13; 1 John 4:6, 5:6)

Spirit of understanding (Isaiah 11:2; Luke 24:45; Ephesians 1:18; Colossians 1:9)

Spirit of wisdom (Deuteronomy 34:9; Isaiah 11:2; Ephesians 1:17; Colossians 1:9)

Spirit of your Father (Matthew 10:20)

Spirit who convicts (John 16:7–11)

Spirit who groans (Romans 8:26)

Spirit who lives in us (John 14:20; Romans 8:11; 1 Corinthians 3:16; Galatians 2:20; 2 Timothy 1:14; 1 John 3:24, 4:12–16)

Spirit who sanctifies (Romans 15:16; 2 Thessalonians 2:13; 1 Peter 1:2)

Spirit who speaks (Acts 8:29, 10:19, 11:12, 13:2, 20:23, 21:11, and 28:25; Galatians 4:6; Revelation 2:7, 2:11, 2:17, 2:29, and 22:17)

Spirit who teaches (guides) (Nehemiah 9:20; Luke 12:12; John 14:26, 16:13; 1 Corinthians 2:13; 1 John 2:27)

Spirit who testifies (witnesses) (John 15:26; Acts 5:30–32; Romans 8:16; Hebrews 2:4; 1 John 5:7–8)

Spirit, eternal (Ecclesiastes 3:11; Galatians 6:8; Hebrews 9:14)

Spirit, good (Nehemiah 9:20; Psalm 143:10)

Spirit, Holy (Psalm 51:11; Isaiah 63:10–11; Matthew 1:18–20, 3:11, and 28:19; Luke 4:1; John 20:22; Acts 2:38; 1 Corinthians 6:19; Ephesians 4:30; Hebrews 10:15; Jude 1:20)

Spirit, one (1 Corinthians 12:13; Ephesians 2:18; 4:4)

Spirits, seven (sevenfold spirit; perfect) (Isaiah 11:2; Revelation 1:4, 3:1, 4:5, and 5:6)

Splendor (1 Chronicles 16:27; Job 37:22; Psalms 96:6, 104:1, and 145:5; Isaiah 35:1–2, 63:1; Habakkuk 3:4)

Spring of the water of life (Revelation 21:6)

Spring(s) of living water (Psalm 114:8; Isaiah 35:7, 41:18, and 49:10; Jeremiah 2:13, 17:13; John 4:13–14; Revelation 7:17, 21:6)

Star (Matthew 2:1–2)

Star, bright and morning (2 Peter 1:19; Revelation 2:28, 22:16)

Star, Jacob's (Numbers 24:17)

Stone cut without hands (Daniel 2:34, 2:45)

Stone laid in Zion (Isaiah 28:16; Romans 9:33; 1 Peter 2:6)

Stone of Jacob (Genesis 28:18–22)

Stone of stumbling (Isaiah 8:13–14; Romans 9:32–33; 1 Peter 2:8)

Stone, chosen of God (1 Peter 2:4, 2:6)

Stone, living (1 Peter 2:4)

Stone, precious (1 Peter 2:6–7)

Stone, rejected (Psalm 118:22; Matthew 21:42; Mark 12:10; Luke 20:17–18; Acts 4:11; 1 Peter 2:7)

Stone, rolled back (Matthew 28:2; Mark 16:2–5; Luke 24:1–2; John 20:1)

Stone, tried, tested (Isaiah 28:16)

Stone, white (Revelation 2:17)

Stones, memorial (Joshua 4)

Stranger (Matthew 25:35)

Streams (Psalms 42:1, 65:9; Isaiah 32:1–2, 35:5–6, and 44:3–4; Jeremiah 31:9; John 7:38)

Strength (Exodus 15:2; Psalms 18:1, 22:19, 28:7–8, 46:1, 59:9, 59:16–17, and 118:14; Isaiah 12:2; Jeremiah 16:19; Habakkuk 3:16–19; Ephesians 6:10)

Stronghold (2 Samuel 22:3; Psalms 9:9, 18:2, 27:1, 37:39, 43:2, 52:7, and 144:2; Joel 3:16)

Sun of righteousness (Psalm 84:11; Malachi 4:2; Matthew 17:2)

Sun, rising (2 Samuel 23:3–4; Hosea 6:3; Luke 1:76–79)

Superior (Ephesians 1:21; Philippians 2:9–11; Hebrews 1:4, 8:6)

Supper, Lord's (Matthew 26:26–29; Mark 14:22–25; Luke 22:20; 1 Corinthians 11:20–26)

Supper, Wedding (John 2:1–11; Revelation 19:9)

Support (2 Samuel 22:19; Psalms 18:18, 94:18)

Surety (guarantee, ensure) (Job 17:3; Psalm 119:122; Hebrews 7:22)

Sustainer (Nehemiah 9:21; Psalms 3:5, 18:35, 54:4, 55:22, 89:21, 119:116, and 145:14; Isaiah 46:4; Hebrews 1:3)

Sword (Genesis 3:24; Deuteronomy 33:29; Psalms 7:12, 17:13, and 45:3; Isaiah 27:1, 49:2, and 66:16; Jeremiah 47:6–7; Ezekiel 21; Matthew 10:34; Hebrews 4:12; Revelation 1:16, 2:12, and 2:16)

Sword of the Spirit (Ephesians 6:17)

T

Tablets of stone (covenant) (Exodus 24:12, 31:18, 34:1–4, and 34:28; Deuteronomy 4:13, 9:10–15, and 10:1–5; Hebrews 9:4)

Teacher (Matthew 8:19, 19:16, and 26:18; Mark 4:38, 9:38; Luke 6:40, 19:39, and 22:11; John 1:38, 3:2, 11:28, 13:13, and 20:16)

Temple (for the name of the Lord) (1 Kings 6; Ezra 3:10–13, 6:15–22; Psalms 11:4, 48:9; Malachi 3:1; John 2:18–22; Revelation 7:15, 11:19, and 21:22)

Temple (tabernacle) of testimony (Numbers 1:47–53; Revelation 15:5)

Tent (of meeting) (Exodus 27:21, 33:7–11, and 40:34–35; 2 Chronicles 1:3–6, 5:5; Psalm 61:4; Acts 15:16; Revelation 7:15)

Testimony of Jesus Christ (John 8:14; Revelation 1:2, 1:9, 12:17, 19:10, and 22:20)

Throne of a priest (Zechariah 6:13)

Throne of ancient of days (Daniel 7:9–10; Revelation 1:4)

Throne of David (2 Samuel 7:16; Psalm 89:35–37; Isaiah 9:6–7; Luke 1:32; Acts 2:29–30)

Throne of Father (Matthew 20:20–23; Revelation 3:21)

Throne of flaming fire (Daniel 7:9)

Throne of grace (Hebrews 4:16)

Throne of heaven (heavenly) (Psalms 11:4, 103:19, and 123:1; Isaiah 66:1; Matthew 5:34, 23:22; Acts 7:49)

Throne of honor (1 Samuel 2:8)

Throne of judgment (Psalm 9:7; Daniel 7:9–10; Revelation 20:11–15)

Throne of living water (Revelation 22:1)

Throne of love (Proverbs 20:28; Isaiah 16:5)

Throne of righteousness and justice (Psalms 89:14, 97:2; Proverbs 16:12, 25:5)

Throne of sapphire (Exodus 24:9–11; Ezekiel 1:26, 10:1)

Throne of Son (Luke 1:31–32; Acts 2:30; Revelation 3:21)

Throne of the Lamb (Revelation 5:6, 7:9–11, 14:1–3, and 22:3)

Throne of the LORD (God) (1 Kings 22:19; 1 Chronicles 29:23; Isaiah 6:1; Hebrews 1:8, 12:2; Revelation 7:9–12, 19:4, and 22:3)

Throne of the Majesty in heaven (Hebrews 8:1)

Throne, eternal (2 Samuel 7:13–16; 1 Chronicles 17:12–14; Psalms 45:6, 89:35–37; Lamentations 5:19; Hebrews 1:8; Revelation 1:4–5, 4:9–10, 5:13, and 21:4–5)

Throne, glorious (Isaiah 63:15; Jeremiah 14:21, 17:12; Matthew 19:28, 25:31)

Throne, great white (Revelation 20:11)

Throne, holy (Psalm 47:8; Isaiah 63:15)

Tongues of fire (Matthew 3:11–12; Acts 2:3)

Torch, blazing (Genesis 15:17)

Tower of deliverance (strong tower) (Psalm 61:3; Proverbs 18:10)

Trainer, of my hands (2 Samuel 22:35; Psalms 18:34, 144:1)

Trap (snare) (Isaiah 8:14–15)

Treasure, hidden (Deuteronomy 33:19; Isaiah 33:5–6; Matthew 13:44; 2 Corinthians 4:7)

Treasures of wisdom and knowledge (Colossians 2:2–3)

Tree of life (Genesis 2:9, 3:22; Revelation 2:7, 22:2, and 22:14)

Tree, apple (Song of Solomon 2:3)

Tree, green pine (Hosea 14:8)

Truth (John 1:14, 1:17, 8:32, 14:6, and 17:17)

U

Unchanging One (Psalm 102:26–27; Malachi 3:6; Hebrews 1:12, 13:8; James 1:17)

Unknown name (Revelation 19:12)

Upright One (Deuteronomy 32:4; Psalms 25:8, 92:15; Isaiah 26:7)

V

Victory (Romans 8:37; 1 Corinthians 15:57; 1 John 5:3–5)

Vine, true (John 15:1, 15:5)

W

Wall of fire (Zechariah 2:5)

Walls of salvation (Isaiah 26:1, 60:18; Revelation 21:12–18)

Warrior (Exodus 14:14, 15:3; Deuteronomy 1:30, 3:22, and 20:4; Joshua 23:3, 23:10; Nehemiah 4:20; Isaiah 42:13; Jeremiah 20:11)

Watcher of men (Job 7:20, 33:11; Psalms 32:8, 33:14, 121, and 145:20; Jeremiah 31:10, 31:28)

Water (Isaiah 35:6, 55:1; Ezekiel 36:25, 47:1–12; Matthew 3:13–17; John 3:5, 19:34; 1 Peter 3:20–21; 1 John 5:6–8)

Water of life (Revelation 21:6, 22:1, and 22:17)

Waters, living (Jeremiah 2:13, 17:13; Zechariah 14:8; John 4:10, 7:37–39; Revelation 7:17)

Way (Isaiah 55:8–9; John 14:6; Acts 9:2, 19:9, 19:23, 22:4, 24:14, and 24:22; Ephesians 2:18)

Way of holiness (Isaiah 35:8)

Way, everlasting (Psalm 139:24; Habakkuk 3:6; John 14:1–4)

Way, new and living (Hebrews 10:20)

Wells of salvation (Isaiah 12:3)

Whisper (1 Kings 19:12; Job 26:14)

Who is, who was, who is to come (Revelation 1:8, 4:8, 11:17, and 16:5)

Wind (Ezekiel 37:9; John 3:8; Acts 2:2)

Wine (Proverbs 9:2, 9:5; Song of Solomon 1:2; Isaiah 55:1; Matthew 26:27–29; Mark 14:23–25; Luke 22:17–18, 22:20; 1 Corinthians 11:25–26)

Wings (Ruth 2:12; Malachi 4:2; Matthew 23:37)

Wings, eagles (Exodus 19:4; Deuteronomy 32:11)

Wisdom of God (Isaiah 33:6; 1 Corinthians 1:24, 1:30; Ephesians 3:10)

Witness (faithful and true) (Genesis 31:50; 1 Samuel 12:5; Job 16:19; Isaiah 55:4; Jeremiah 29:23, 42:5; 2 Corinthians 1:23; 1 Thessalonians 2:5; Revelation 1:5, 3:14)

Wonderful (Job 42:1–3; Psalms 119:18, 139:5–6; Isaiah 9:6, 28:29)

Word (God said) (Genesis 1:3; Deuteronomy 8:3, 30:14; Matthew 4:4; John 1:1)

Word made flesh (John 1:14)

Word of God (Revelation 19:13)

Word of life (1 John 1:1)

Word (teaching) of truth (Psalms 25:4–5, 86:11, and 119:160; John 1:14, 1:17, 8:31–32, 17:8, and 17:17; Ephesians 1:13; James 1:18)

Word, eternal (Psalms 119:89, 119:152, and 119:160; Isaiah 40:8; Matthew 24:35; 1 Peter 1:23–25)

Words, trustworthy (2 Samuel 7:28; Psalms 19:7, 111:7–8, and 119:138; Revelation 21:5, 22:6)

Worm (Psalm 22:6)

Worthy of praise (2 Samuel 22:4; 1 Chronicles 16:25; Psalms 18:3, 48:1, and 145:3; Revelation 4:11, 5:2, and 5:12)

Wrath of God Almighty (Deuteronomy 29:28; Psalms 7:11, 110:5; Isaiah 63:1–6; John 3:36; Romans 1:18, 2:5–8, and 12:19; Ephesians 5:6; 1 Thessalonians 1:10)

Wrath of the Lamb (Revelation 6:16–17)

Wrath, cup of (Isaiah 51:17–23; Jeremiah 25:15–17; Matthew 20:22–23; Mark 14:36; John 18:11; Revelation 14:9–10, 16:19)

Wrath, winepress of (Isaiah 63:1–6; Lamentations 1:15; Revelation 14:19–20, 19:15)

Y

Yes (Isaiah 43:13, 52:6; 2 Corinthians 1:19–20; Revelation 22:20)

Yoke, my (Matthew 11:28–30; 2 Corinthians 6:14; Galatians 5:25; 1 Peter 2:21; 1 John 2:6)

Z

Zeal, zealous (Numbers 25:10–13; 2 Kings 19:31; Psalms 69:9, 119:139; Isaiah 9:7, 26:11, 37:32, 42:13, and 59:17; Ezekiel 5:13, 36:5, and 39:25; John 2:17)

Zion (Psalms 2:6, 9:11, 50:2, and 76:2; Isaiah 28:16, 51:11, and 51:16; Joel 3:21; Obadiah 1:17, 1:21; Zechariah 8:3; Hebrews 12:22; 1 Peter 2:6; Revelation 14:1)

Bibliography

Arthur, Kay. *To Know Him by Name*. Sisters: Multnomah Books, 1995.

Bell, Robert D. *The Theological Messages of the Old Testament Books*. Greenville: Bob Jones University Press, 2010.

Erickson, Millard J. *Christian Theology*. Grand Rapids: Baker Books, 1998.

Fellows, Andrew. "A Time to Grieve: A Lamentation for the Loss of Lament." A workshop presented at the European Leadership Forum, Wisla, Poland, May 30–June 4, 2015.

Goodrick, Edward W., and John R. Kohlenberger III. *The NIV Exhaustive Concordance*. Grand Rapids: Zondervan Publishing House, 1990.

Grudem, Wayne. *Systematic Theology: An Introduction to Biblical Doctrine*. Grand Rapids: Zondervan Publishing House, 1994.

International Bible Society. *The Holy Bible*, New International Version. Grand Rapids: Zondervan Bible Publishers, 1984.

Large, James. *Titles and Symbols of Christ: 280 Clear and Powerful Images of Christ Revealed in the Scriptures*. Chattanooga: AMG Publishers, 1994.

Lockman Foundation. *New American Standard Bible*. La Habra: Foundation Press Publications, 1973.

Lockyer, Herbert. *All the Divine Names and Titles in the Bible*. Grand Rapids: Zondervan, 1975.

MacArthur, John, John Eldredge, Max Lucado, Charles R. Swindoll, Sheila Walsh, Billy Graham, Kathy Troccoli, Dee Brestin, Anne Graham Lotz. *Jesus*. Nashville: W Publishing Group, 2004.

Muller-Simhofer, Markus. "MindNode, Delightful Mind Mapping." Vienna: Ideas on Canvas, 2016. Version 2.3.2 used by permission.

Packer, J.I. *Knowing God*. Downers Grove: InterVarsity Press, 1973.

Patterson, Ben. *Waiting: Finding Hope When God Seems Silent*. Downers Grove: InterVarsity Press, 1989.

Pennebaker, James W. *Writing to Heal: A Guided Journal for Recovering from Trauma and Emotional Upheaval.* Oakland: New Harbinger, 2004.

Peterson, Eugene H. *A Long Obedience in the Same Direction: Discipleship in an Instant Society.* Downers Grove: InterVarsity Press, 2000.

Peterson, Eugene H. *Run with the Horses: The Quest for Life at Its Best.* Downers Grove: InterVarsity Press, 2009.

Piper, John. *Let the Nations Be Glad!: The Supremacy of God in Missions.* Grand Rapids: Baker Academic, 2010.

Piper, John. *Think: The Life of the Mind and the Love of God.* Wheaton: Crossway, 2010.

Richards, Larry. *Every Name of God in the Bible.* Nashville: Thomas Nelson Publishers, 2001.

Rodgers, Beverly and Tom Rodgers. "Neurological insights into emotional reactivity and relational conflict." *Christian Counseling Connection*, Vol.19, Issue 4, December 2013.

Spangler, Ann. *Praying the Names of God: A Daily Guide.* Grand Rapids: Zondervan, 2004.

Spangler, Ann. *Praying the Names of Jesus: A Daily Guide.* Grand Rapids: Zondervan, 2006.

Thompson, Frank Charles. *The New Chain-Reference Bible*, 4th edition, King James Version. Indianapolis: B. B. Kirkbride Bible Co., Inc., 1964.

Tournier, Paul. *A Listening Ear: Reflections on Christian Care Giving.* Minneapolis: Augsburg Publishing House, 1986.

Towns, Elmer L. *365 Ways to Know God: Devotional Readings on the Names of God.* Ventura: Regal Books, 2004.

Internet Resources

Buzan, Tony. "Maximize the Potential of Your Brain: Tony Buzan Talks about Mind Mapping." Accessed December 2016." http://www.buzan.com.au.

Dictionary.com./Thesaurus.com. Accessed August 2013–February 2017. http://www.thesaurus.com.

Langberg, Dr. Diane. "Fellowship of His Suffering: Ground Zero, 2010." Accessed June 15, 2015. http://www.dianelangberg.com.

About the Author

Caranita Wolsieffer is a member of the American Association of Christian Counselors and the Italian Association of Marriage and Family Counselors. She publishes articles in counseling journals and mission magazines. Graduates of Johnson University in Knoxville, Tn., she and her husband were recipients of the 2014 Alumni Award. Her Masters from Bob Jones University and SICOF in Rome qualify her as a small group leader and a supervisor. She is the co-founder and president of the non-profit counseling association Recrea (www.recrea.it) in southern Italy where she and her husband work for the Italy for Christ Mission (www. italyforchrist.org). She conducts workshops on trauma and shame and spoke at the 2016 International Commission on Couple and Family Relations. Her passion for God's Names grew from her own personal experience of childhood trauma that impacted her walk of faith. She draws inspiration from her husband's courageous battle with disabilities and how he reaches out to others, no matter what.

Illustrator's biography:

Tony has spent most of his career as an accomplished caricature artist, accumulating over 10,000 hours of drawing practice as well as proximity to numerous professional artists and art forms around the world. In 2014 Tony received several awards at the International Society of Caricature Artists Convention in Reno, NV, including 1st place in Black and White Technique and placing as one of the top 10 caricature artists of the year (7th place). In addition to his award-winning caricatures, Tony studied studio art through classes at the University of Tennessee and Pellissippi State Community College in Knoxville, TN, as well as the Los Angeles Academy of Figurative Art and Schoolism online. His fine art style—a blend of realism, surrealism, and abstract art—attracts collectors from all over the US and can be seen publicly during his annual group and solo exhibitions. You can find more of his work at www. tonysobota.com.

Printed in the United States
By Bookmasters